LEAD ROPES DON'T LEAD HORSES

and 49 other thoughts for horse lovers

CAT ENRIGHT & LISA WYSOCKY

TITLES

Published by
Cool Titles
439 N. Canon Dr., Suite 200
Beverly Hills, CA 90210
www.cooltitles.com

The Library of Congress Cataloging-in-Publication Data Applied For

Lisa Wysocky
Lead Ropes Don't Lead Horses: and 49 Other Thoughts for Horse Lovers

p.   cm
ISBN 978-1-935270-61-4
1. Horses 2. Horse Behavior 3. Horse Training I. Title
2023

Copyright 2023 by Lisa Wysocky
All Rights Reserved
including the right of reproduction in whole or in part in any form.

Printed in the United States of America

3 5 7 9 10 8 6 4 2

For interviews, information regarding distribution, or special discounts to the trade or for bulk purchases, contact cindy@cooltitles.com

Dedication

Since the authors could not agree
on any other dedication, this is for the horses.
Always, it is for the horses.

Table of Contents

About the Cover 1
Introduction 3
Contest 6
About the Horses... 9
About the People 15
Horse Behavior 18
Horse Care 68
Horse Training 85
Riding... 102
Acknowledgments 128
Author Bios 130

About the Cover

Lex, our cover model, is a nineteen-year-old, 16.2 hand therapy horse who weighs 1,550 pounds. And, he probably has the longest ears of any horse in the entire world, but in an effort to only promote positive body images, no one mentions either his weight or his ears when he is in hearing distance.

His rare coloring is called silver dapple bay, which is only seen in a few breeds, including the Shire, a draft breed, and the Shetland, a pony breed. We'll let you guess whether he gets his coloring from the Shetland or the Shire. Actually, Lex is a Thoroughbred/Shire/Belgian cross who is three-quarters Thoroughbred, although he doesn't look it.

Before Lex ended up at Colby's Army, the therapeutic riding program that Lisa runs in Ashland City, Tennessee, he was a trail horse, and also a hunter/jumper lesson horse. Somewhere out there on the internet are a few cute videos of Lex teaching eight- and nine-year-old kids to jump. He doesn't jump much anymore, but when he gets excited in the pasture he has been known to stand up on his hind legs and hop around in a circle. When he is sternly told to, "Get down!" he comes down so hard he shakes the ground enough that the neighbors sometimes call to see if everyone at Colby's Army felt the earthquake, too.

Lex is a worrier who tries so very hard to get everything right. To relieve stress, he likes to annoy to his pasture-mates and also likes to put his front feet into the hundred-gallon water trough and then lean back and tip it over. Fun times! In spring his favorite activity is to splash in mud puddles, and in summer he lives to be hosed down with cold water. Lex would happily stand under a sprinkler all day if he could.

People fascinate Lex, and he is so curious about humans and what we ask him to do. Other than being annoying, pretending to be a Lipizzan, and tipping over water troughs, his only really bad habit is that he sometimes likes to chew on his lead rope. That's why he was chosen to be our cover model. It was a challenge, though, to get him to walk the direction needed for the background to work on the cover while holding the lead rope in his mouth. We also found early on that he did not at all like purple or red lead ropes. Those he quickly spit out. But he liked the blue and a few multi-colored ropes very much.

Lex was so good during several photo shoots, and was present and engaged for longer periods of time than we ever expected. Many thanks to Callie Rogers and Darcy Whitcomb for their help in getting Lex photo ready, and for their help during the shoots. And of course, to Lex, the world's very best long-eared, water-loving, draft cross, lead-rope-eating therapy horse.

Introduction

Over the course of the past five Cat Enright mystery adventures written by my friend, Lisa Wysocky, many readers have asked me about my thoughts on horses and training. So many, that I asked Lisa if she would collaborate with me on this project, because seriously, I have no idea how to write a book. And, there is the fact that I am a fictional character, at least in the minds of some people. To others, including Lisa, I am very real.

After a few (okay many, *many*) fumbling attempts, we gained traction with the horse tips that are found at the end of some of the chapters in the mysteries, and expanded those thoughts. Then we said, "Nah," threw out some of the topics, and brought a few new ones in. Finally, we organized them into sections of horse behavior, horse care, horse training, and riding, because most of us do love to ride.

While we hadn't planned it, we also included some illustrative stories that involve people who are featured in some of the mysteries that Lisa writes. These includes my foster son, Bubba Henley; my riding student and roommate, Darcy Whitcomb; and Jon Gardner. Jon is hard to define. He is, or was, my barn manager, right hand, and sort of boyfriend, but all of that is fluid at the moment.

Anyway, the ideas and thoughts are mine, and mostly involve things people do or don't do with horses (or possibly it's the people themselves) that absolutely drive me nuts. The presentation of the information is Lisa's, though, and she's far more tolerant of people than I am, so it is a good collaboration, I think. I hope you think so, too.

Unfortunately, Sally Blue and the rest of my horses refused, yes *refused*, to participate in the photo shoots for this book. Sally's owner, Agnes Temple, who says she can commune with Sally from as far away as her home in Louisville, Kentucky, said the horses in my barn did not want the publicity that comes with their photos being seen by so many people. Lisa's horses at Colby's Army had no such thoughts and cooperated fully. Her horses, apparently, are not divas.

—Cat Enright
August 2023

Cindy Johnson, our editor and publisher, first had the idea for Cat Enright to write a non-fiction book about horses. But, it took Cat and me a while to figure out how to do that, because really, how do you co-author a book with a fictional character?

As many fiction authors will tell you, characters become (sort of) real to us. So in a way, this was like co-authoring a book with a friend. In writing the Cat Enright equestrian mysteries, Cat's thoughts and opinions do not always coincide with mine, and we do argue about it some. Or, as Cat yells inside my head, "I'm not arguing. I'm explaining why I am correct." Sigh.

But, the process was the same here as it is with the mysteries. Cat and I are close on most thoughts, but we diverge on a few others. Somehow here we were able to meet in the middle. Mostly her middle, but who's counting?

Cat and I do both think the information presented is important for those who love horses. If you're not a horse lover, though, much of the information can be translated to your interactions with people, so there is something here for you, too. And maybe by the end of the book you'll be intrigued enough to want to learn more about horses.

Lastly, while this is a non-fiction book, you will also get a few bits of inside information and back story about Cat and her friends that you might not have known before.

Read, learn, enjoy!

—Lisa Wysocky

August 2023

Contest!

Lisa and I both love contests, so we just had to include one here, even though it took us a while to think of one. But eventually we did. Throughout the book, you will occasionally see a word in the middle of the text that is underlined. It will appear out of the blue, like magic.

Best to write those words down somewhere: in your phone, on your tablet, on a piece of notebook paper, but probably not on your hand like Bubba does because you'll have to bathe at some point before you gather up all the words, and then all your hard work will be lost.

After you have found all the words, sort through them to form one or two sentences about horses. Or, maybe the sentence(s) are about my friends and me. You'll have to figure it out, and, you must use all the words. Those who can do those things can then email the sentence(s) to: cooltitleseditor@gmail.com, and Lisa or I, or someone, will send you a kindle or epub version of any one of the first five Cat Enright mysteries of your choice. But, you must do so before December 30, 2024.

Then, one grand prize winner, drawn at random, will win one print copy set of all of the Cat Enright books. How cool is that? Happy word hunting.

—Cat

Spike is very intrigued about a contest! If he wins, he requests peppermints as his prize.

About the Horses

Throughout the book you'll see a few photos of horses, and Lisa and I wanted to share a little about them in hopes the information will give you more insight into the stories they help illustrate. We've already mentioned Lex. If you skipped over the About the Cover section earlier, you might want to go back and skim through that.

You will also see some photos of Tessie. At the time of this writing Tessie is a 15.2 hand, twenty-two-year-old chestnut Belgian/Quarter Horse cross who in a previous life was an Amish driving horse. She also spent a brief period of time as a trail horse. She is the herd leader at Colby's Army and is such a wonderful therapy horse that she was awarded the Professional Association of Therapeutic Horsemanship's (PATH) Region Five Equine of the Year award. No one reminds her of that, though, because when she won the award everyone started to bring her treats and she became insufferably entitled.

By and by she got over it, and went back to excelling at making ugly faces at the three boys in her herd and expecting her humans to stand around and scratch her all day. Mostly, her expectations are met. She always checks out strangers who come to visit and absolutely will not allow the boys to engage with new people until she has checked them up and down. She also is a versatile therapy horse, and can serve as a first horse for a loud, emotional five-year-old all the way through to teaching more advanced riders to canter.

Quincy is a twenty-four-year-old, dark bay, 16 hand, solid-colored registered Appaloosa. We know. He looks like a Thoroughbred, but as far back as we can trace his lineage there is no such breeding anywhere in his pedigree. Go figure. Quincy is the kind of guy who absolutely does not want to make any decisions about his own life. Get a drink of water . . . or not? Stand in the sun, or the shade? Someone please tell him what to do.

You have probably figured out by now that Quincy is the low man on the totem pole when it comes to the horse herd. But, he is

Tessie and Quincy are best friends.

the sweetest and kindest horse who ever lived. Before he was donated to Colby's Army, Quincy was a third-level Dressage horse, a low-level event horse, and a 4-H project horse, so he's just about done it all. But he is also a cribber and has a long-ago barbed-wire injury that sometimes makes his right front pastern ache.

All of this adds up to the fact that, no, Quincy as an elderly, arthritic cribber is not perfect, but that lets people in the therapeutic riding program (and volunteers and staff, too) know that if everyone can love the imperfect Quincy, maybe people can love their own imperfect selves. Quincy has been retired from riding, but helps train volunteers and lesson participants to groom, lead, and ground drive, and he is very informative to watch when doing herd observation activities.

Finally, we have Spike. Spike is a gray, 16.2 hand, nineteen-year-old registered Quarter Horse, probably an appendix, which means since we know who his sire was, that his mother was probably a Thoroughbred. Before he became a therapy horse, Spike and his human family spent a lot of time riding in the Black Hills of South Dakota, and in the Missouri Ozarks. He finds people fascinating and always has his nose right in the middle of things when people fix the fence, clean out the water trough, or rake up poop in the paddock. He likes to "help." He's an awesome independent canter horse who can also handle on-lead therapeutic lessons.

So, for photos we have Lex with the big ears (silver dapple bay), Tessie (chestnut with a white stripe down her face), Quincy (dark bay with a star and snip), and Spike (gray/white). We hope you enjoy their photos.

You will also hear me talk about some of the horses in my barn, the horses who refused to be photographed. Lisa and I initially mentioned their basic information the first time they were discussed in the book, but decided we could give them more detail here.

We'll start with Sally Blue, because everything seems to revolve around her. She's a young, registered Appaloosa mare, 15.2, red roan with white across her hips. Stocky in build, she excels in everything she tries—including the solving of crimes. Well, at least some people think so. The jury is still out on that issue for me. She might just be a very intuitive mare. Or, maybe she really is psychic like her owner, Agnes Temple, keeps telling me. I will say, she often does display very weird behavior that might possibly be construed as delivering clues.

Peter's Pride is a tall, thinner black Appaloosa gelding with dime-sized white spots all over his body. He is owned by my riding student, Darcy Whitcomb, and they are a good match. Petey can be playful, and likes to hold his lead rope in his mouth and lead himself down the aisle. He would have been great on the cover, had he chosen to cooperate. Instead of a cover model, Petey is a great all-around youth horse and a wonderful companion for Darcy. Oh, and his age. Well, he's older, but not ancient.

Glamour Girl (Gigi) is a chestnut Appaloosa filly who I sometimes think doesn't have even the teensiest brain cell inside her head. She lives in the moment and enjoys absolutely every experience very much, even if it makes life frustrating for the humans around her. She has won a national championship at halter, and is currently turned out to grow up some, since she found ground driving and the process of saddling way too much fun. I don't know about you, but if I'm going to be on top of a horse, I like there to be a bit of steadiness underneath me. She'll get there, just not today.

Another Appaloosa, Ringo, is owned by a Texan named Gusher Black. Before Ringo came to my barn, he had won championships in halter and racing, and my job was to deliver a national or world championship in performance to Ringo and Gusher—which I did, by the way. After that, Ringo went on to training in distance riding and was a winner there, making him one of the very few four-medallion Appaloosas. I am really happy to have been a small part of his rising success.

Hillbilly Bob, is a 15.3 hand bay Appaloosa gelding with a big white blanket and lots of spots. He was owned by my orthopedic physician, which turned out to be advantageous since I find I often need to have such a doctor on speed dial. Bob is one of those boring bombproof types. He rarely makes a mistake and often wins classes in competition by default. Even though he is never the flashiest in the class, sooner or later the other horses will bobble, and Bob, due to his plodding steadiness, will take home <u>the</u> blue ribbon.

But, Bob has won just about everything there is to win, and Doc wants to move up to something new, so he gave Bob to me, and my foster son, Bubba, is now riding and showing him.

There will be a few other horses mentioned throughout the book, but these are the main ones. I really wish you could see them, but they insist they want to retain at least some of their privacy and I have to respect that.

About the People

As with the horses, Lisa and I decided to first mention here the people we will most often reference in telling stories that make a point, rather than give big dumps of their information farther into the book. Here's where Lisa and I had a tiny disagreement: who to include first? I didn't want any of my friends to feel slighted because they were lumped into the middle of the pack, so to speak, but we finally settled on an alphabetical order.

If you are a fan of the mysteries that Lisa writes about my adventures, you will be familiar with the people below, but maybe you will learn something new about them. If you haven't read any of the mysteries, well, I'm glad you're reading this book, and I absolutely promise we will get to the information I have to share about horses very soon.

It's ironic that Agnes Temple comes first, since she is such a force of nature. A little of Agnes goes a long way, but I love her dearly. Agnes is a seventy-ish former cheerleader who has a big heart. And, thanks to her three deceased husbands, whose ashes she carries with her in her purse, she has lots of money. She owns Sally Blue and has owned other horses in my barn over the decade or so I have known her. Agnes comes complete with a caregiver, because really, someone has to keep her in line. Lars is an almost seven-foot-tall very fit black man who mostly dresses in form-fitting black leather vests and pants—with lots of gold chains to cover up where his shirt should be. Agnes lives in an upscale condo in Louisville, Kentucky. Recently, she acquired a pot-bellied pig named Arabella. Agnes and Lars stay busy trying to keep Arabella hidden from the condo board, because of course what would Agnes do with all of Arabella's sparkly pink tutus if Arabella didn't live with Agnes in the condo?

Bubba Henley used to be my neighbor two houses over. He's twelve now and has become my foster son. This is only after his good-for-nothing horse trainer dad, Hill Henley, shot the toe off an Alabama state trooper after Hill was stopped for illegally transporting stolen CDs across a state line. I swear that when Hill took his IQ test the results must have been negative. That might be why Bubba's mother took off for parts unknown years ago, and why Bubba ended up with me. Bubba was a budding juvenile delinquent but has settled down some since he's been under my roof. Now he just likes to spend time riding Bob and thinking up ways to prank people. While he thinks pranks are hysterically funny, others of us do not. His dad will be in jail for a bit, since while incarcerated he was also part of a cell phone scheme to steal people's data, so I think Bubba will be with me for a few years yet. I'm actually surprisingly happy about that.

Carole Carson and I are not all that close, but I consider her my best friend. Not sure what that says about me, but I do tend to keep people at arm's length. They say opposites attract and Carole and I could not be more different. She is impossibly tall and thin with luscious dark hair. Before she married country music superstar Keith Carson she was a model, and even now after giving birth to four kids, I think she is the most beautiful woman I have ever seen. Fortunately, Carole is down-to-earth, laid back, and intelligent, in addition to being a great mom. She is not, sadly, a dedicated horse person, although I do have hope that will change in the future.

I met Darcy Whitcomb when she was thirteen and started taking riding lessons from me. It didn't take long for me to see that while her divorced parents had pots of money, they didn't have much time for their daughter. Darcy does well at the horse shows, but not as well as she could if she fully applied herself. The summer before her senior year in high school she announced that she was moving in with me, and after a bit of tense negotiation with her dad, it came to be. Now she is studying equine management in college and hopes one day to be a therapeutic riding instructor.

If Carole Carson is the most beautiful woman I have ever seen, her husband Keith is the most beautiful man on the planet. How did I ever get so lucky as to have them move in next door to me? I not only get to peek through the shrubbery that divides our properties when he washes his boat in his swim trunks, I got to teach him how to ride for a music video. Plus, there was that time when he saved my life by doing mouth-to-mouth resuscitation. I will regret to my dying day that I was unconscious at the time.

Hill Henley comes from a long-standing, prominent Cheatham County, Tennessee family, but over the years they have declined in status to the point that calling Hill white trash would be considered polite. Before he went to prison, his profession was as a trainer of Tennessee Walking Horses, but in fact, he cowed every horse he had into submission. He's crude, foul-mouthed, and belligerent. I always try to find something nice to say about others, but with Hill, this gives me quite the dilemma since I don't want to lie. Hmm . . . Well, he's tall. He has that going for him. Oh, and he has quite the amazing son in Bubba. There!

Describing Jon Gardner is like describing the color blue. There are many shades and the color means different things to different people. But Lisa says I have to try, so here are a few words: friend, right hand, barn manager, loyal, trustworthy, sometime boyfriend, mysterious, quiet. I look at the words and know they give you nothing, really, about Jon. But it's all I have right now. My feelings for him are complicated, and whenever I try to grasp onto them, they slip away. He's awesome with the horses and I am sad that right now we are taking a break from each other.

Horse Behavior

Well, here we go. Here's the part I've been dreading. Lisa says not to worry, that I have good information for you. I hope so. All I know is that the thoughts and ideas that follow work for me. They may not work for you, or for you and your current horse(s), or life in general *now*. But if you tuck the thoughts away, maybe you can trot them out successfully in the future.

This first section is about horse behavior, because I just don't think you can be successful as a rider, or even as a lover of horses, unless you first deepen your understanding of why they act and react as they do.

HUMANS ARE PREDATORS, WHILE HORSES ARE PREY. GIVEN THE CHANCE, A HORSE PREFERS TO RUN FROM DANGER, RATHER THAN FIGHT.

This is what non-horse people don't understand. A horse is not a dog, and cannot be treated as such. Even miniature horses, who are so cute, think, eat, and breathe like the horses they are. A horse is a prey animal, and has a natural instinct to flee from danger. This is because horses are not very well-equipped to fight. They have no horns or antlers, and their teeth are not very sharp. Their best defense is to run away as fast as possible—and they are so good at it they can be gone faster than a toupee in a wind tunnel.

When a horse feels threatened, she can startle, and then run. This is the flight response, and it's a natural instinct that helps a horse survive attack from predators or other danger, such as a tree in the pasture crashing down. As you may have experienced yourself, many things can trigger a horse's flight response, including a loud noise or sudden movement, a strange object, or even an object moved from one side of the barn aisle to the other. A perceived predator, someone walking around the corner of the barn, a sudden gust of wind—all of these situations, and many more, can cause

Tessie is the herd leader and investigates everything to be sure it is safe for her herd, and for her.

your horse to think she would be much safer if she was somewhere else.

This understanding that a horse is constantly thinking about her safety is the key to a successful relationship with any horse. Some horses are very secure in themselves and tolerant of changes in their environment. Others, however, react to every single change—even those we do not initially notice.

When I was in college I was assigned a very skittish yearling Quarter Horse filly to work with. She came in on a truck with a number of other untouched yearlings and wanted nothing to do with people, including me. She was kept *in* a pen by herself, but had friends in other nearby pens so she could see and hear all of them. Her pen, like the others, opened to an alley that led to a round pen, a sixty-foot round pipe corral used to work with horses. Every day I spent time with her to establish leadership in the pen, and after a few days, I was able to get a halter on her. Slowly, she began to trust me and we began grooming and leading exercises.

This filly was still very jumpy, but improving. That is until one day I went to work with her and it was as if we were back at the beginning. She shied away from me and jumped at every little thing. I couldn't figure it out until I started looking at her environment from her perspective. All of the pipe fences were red, as were all of the buckets the horses ate and drank from. Except today, I noticed, the faded red buckets had all been replaced with bright, shiny new ones. That teensy change to a bucket that looked and smelled different than what she had become used to and felt safe with had caused her to be untrusting of her environment, and of me. Her reaction, then, was to run as fast as she could around her pen. After I asked the barn manager if we could change out the new bucket for the old, the filly again felt safe enough to continue to let me work with her.

If you remember nothing else, remember that a horse continually asks herself if she is safe—and acts accordingly.

HORSES ARE ABLE TO FORM CATEGORIES AND GENERALIZE.
People do this all the time, from infancy on. But here's the thing. Horses do, too, and so many of us humans regularly underestimate horse intelligence. Regularly! How frustrating that must be for our horse friends. Those of you who have spent time around horses know how smart they are, and whenever anyone calls a horse stupid, it makes me question their intelligence. Of course, anyone who has met Sally Blue will agree. Some say she is so smart she can even solve crimes.

But to do that, Sally has to be able to put objects and events into categories, and then make sense of them. Don't tell her, but she's not the only horse who can do that. All horses can. They can even see and understand the differences between shapes such as triangles and circles.

This was all confirmed in a small study in 2015, published in the research journal *The Royal Society*, where researchers found horses could tell the difference between two circles that were as little as 14 percent different in size. This means that Sally, and every other horse, really can tell the difference between the medium blue bucket that holds grain, and a slightly smaller blue bucket that also is filled with grain. Agnes asked me to tell you that Sally told her she'd choose the big bucket every time.

Horses can tell differences, just like we do, by using a variety of thinking abilities. Attention to detail, for example. Anyone who has ridden a horse who has frozen in place after catching sight of a stray plastic grocery bag blowing across the field knows that a horse is able to focus her full attention on a single, specific object. This focus and attention helps the horse learn the details of the object, and allows her to categorize it.

For example, in the horse's mind, a large, red ball might be categorized by shape, color, movement, and whether or not the horse perceives it to be safe. And what the horse perceives can be specific to that horse. Just as one child might categorize all dogs as safe, a child who has been bitten by a dog might then see all dogs as unsafe.

I also train an excitable young mare named Gigi, and the staid, older gelding, Bob. Because of their personalities and emotional make-up, Gigi perceives almost everything as exciting and unsafe, and Bob thinks the entire world and everything in it is, well . . . quite boring.

In addition to the personality of the horse, horses also learn from their experiences. These individual life experiences allow a horse to improve his ability to put objects into categories, and to generalize. So, a horse might learn to categorize an object as food, or not food, based on his experience in trying to eat it. The horse might also learn to connect his experience with one food, such as grass, to other kinds of food that are similar, such as hay, which is dried grass. This learned ability allows a horse to quickly identify new foods that are safe, or unsafe, to eat.

The horse also remembers what she has learned. Over time, she can then make assumptions about the relationships between objects and events. We have a large bell at Cat Enright Stables. When we ring the bell, the horses in the pasture and paddocks all come charging over to their gates, because they've learned from past experience that dinner comes after the bell rings, and they know they will be led from their current location, through their gate, to their stall—where there is food.

Well, this is true of all our horses, except Sally Blue. In addition to possibly being able to solve crimes, some say Sally is psychic. Admittedly, she does act oddly at times, but I think she's just a very smart and intuitive mare. Because really, a psychic mare? However,, long before anyone goes out to ring the bell, Sally is waiting at the gate. You can make up your own mind about that.

Because horses are prey animals, the ability to form categories and generalize is important, since it allows a horse to learn and adapt to her environment. This is essential for horses to survive in the wild—and also domestically. It's safe to say that horses use their fine-tuned senses of sight, hearing, smell, and touch (all of which we will get to later) to identify and categorize everything around them.

Throughout this book, we'll talk a lot about the fact that humans are predators and horses are prey. Using all of the above abilities, horses can also learn to tell the difference between a predator and a non-threatening animal or object by its shape and size. We humans cannot possibly understand what it is like to be a prey animal who every few seconds asks himself, "Am I safe?" The ability of the horse to categorize and recognize friends, predators, shapes, and other characteristics of things in their world goes a long way toward helping Sally, and all other horses, answer, "Yes. In this moment, I am safe."

HORSES HAVE EXCELLENT VISION AND CAN SEE OBJECTS THAT ARE VERY FAR AWAY.
Fact: a horse's vision is better than a human's. But if you could ask any horse, she'd tell you that they see differently than humans do. Some people just can't understand that there is a difference between the way we see the world and the way a horse sees it, and I wish these

Lex always processes new visual information thoughtfully.

people could get out of their head and wear their horse's shoes, so to speak, just for a day.

In exploring the differences between the way horses and humans see, we have to start with the eye itself. The horse has a huge eye, as big as eight to nine times that of a human. In fact, they have the largest eye of any land mammal. Isn't that cool? And, because a horse's eyes are located on the side of her head, she has a large field of vision that allows her to see almost all the way around her body. There are two blind spots, though, one directly in front and another directly behind, but generally, a horse can see around herself much better than a human can. I mean, how many of us can actually see the backside of our hips without turning our heads? (Not that most of us would want to.)

A horse's range of vision is another element we humans can't possibly understand. If you get the feeling that when it comes to understanding horses most humans are as dumb as tree stumps, you're right. We are! But just think about not being able to see directly in front of you. A few humans with certain eye diseases may experience this, but most of us do not. Then, imagine seeing almost all the way behind you. Bubba says he is glad humans can't see that far around themselves because it would make it very hard for him to sneak up on people and scare them. Remember that he's twelve and still thinks that sort of thing is funny. Me, not so much.

Because of the eye placement on the sides of her head, a horse also sees one image on the left side of her body, and another image on the right. These separate images mean it's difficult for a horse to gauge depth, so when a horse spooks at a big, scary object half a field away, your horse might think it's much closer—and much more of a threat to her safety than it actually is.

We humans strive for 20/20 vision. Horses usually see in the range of 20/30 to 20/60, so their vision is fairly good, but even 20/30 means a horse has to be 50 percent closer to an object to see it as clearly than a human does.

Here's where a big difference in vision comes into play, and you might have to put on your thinking cap for a minute here. Mammals, including humans and horses, have both cones and rods inside their eyes. Cones help with daylight vision, and rods help with night vision. Daylight: cones. Nighttime: rods. Because of the horse's large eye, the horse's ratio of rods to cones is about twenty rods to one cone, but the ratio for a human is only 9:1.

With so many rods, this means a horse can detect details and motion, even in very low-lighting. As you might imagine, it would be a safety issue for a prey animal if she was unable to see at all times, so it is thought that a horse sees nighttime more as we might see a deep dusk.

Maybe like you, I've gotten caught out on the trail a few times when darkness suddenly set in. But each time the horse I was on got me safely home without missing a step—or a turn—when all I could see was blackness. I'm convinced each horse could see with enough clarity to stay on the trail and not run us into a tree or off a cliff. We spend a lot of time getting our horses to trust us, but part of that means us being smart enough to know when to trust our horses. When it comes to night vision, I will trust the horse every single time.

In addition to rods there are the cones, and these cones sense color. Humans have three kinds of cones, so we see a full spectrum of red, yellow-green, and blue light. But horses only have two kinds of cones: blue and yellow. Because of this, horses see blue and green, and variations of the two colors, but do not see much in the way of red or shades of red that include orange and pink, or most yellows or darker purples.

That is why most of my arena equipment is painted various shades of blue, green, and lavender. Interestingly, particularly in our covered arena, my horses often trip over the few poles we occasionally paint another color, sometimes in preparation for a trail or obstacle competition.

The horse's big eye also means that a horse cannot adjust quickly from sun to shade, and vice versa. The eye needs time, as much as several minutes sometimes, to allow for a change from bright sun to shade.

A few years back I was leading staid, unflappable Bob into our barn and he spooked so badly he almost knocked me over. "What the—?" I thought. Well, I won't tell you what I actually thought, because that would be unseemly. Suffice it to say the thought was not a pleasant one.

Bob settled down right away and I looked to our right, since Bob had jumped left, into me, and away from the apparent big, scary monster. Leaning against the wooden barn wall was a wooden pallet. It hadn't been there when we passed the area earlier, but Jon had temporarily placed it there while Bob and I were out riding. Coming in from the sunny outdoors to the dimmer light in the barn, Bob's large eye could not adjust in time and Bob could not see clearly. He sensed something out of the ordinary, and his prey animal instincts kicked in and he jumped into me. Well, not into me personally. I just happened to be in the way. But Bob trusts me and when I calmly said, "Whoa," he stopped and trusted me to be his leader and keep him safe. Really, it is such an honor whenever a horse trusts you with his life.

Finally, each horse is an individual, and like people, some see better than others. *Equus* magazine has reported that roughly 23 percent of domestic horses are nearsighted, which means they don't see details clearly until they get very close to an object. And, roughly 43 percent of horses are farsighted, and are able to make out details only as they get farther away from an object. These differences affect how well an individual horse may do with specific activities, and how they respond to visual stimuli.

And like us, an older horse may not see with as much clarity as a younger horse. So, the next time you become frustrated because your horse won't walk over a tarp, or is spooky on the trail, remember to consider how your horse sees the world differently than you, and try to see your small corner of the world through the eyes of your horse. Only then can you begin to problem solve, and understand why your horse is resistant to doing or behaving as you ask.

LIKE SOME PEOPLE, SOME HORSES ARE CLAUSTROPHOBIC.
Full disclosure: I've been kidnapped a few times. I've been drugged and dumped into a dumpster, and tied up and thrown into the back of a pickup truck—with a cover over the bed.

Quincy does not have personal space issues, but many other horses do.

That's probably why I get a teensy bit claustrophobic in small, tight, dark spaces—because I've had bad experiences in them. Many horses feel the same way, especially inside horse trailers. Anyone who has ever tried to load a horse without success knows that sometimes you just can't convince a twelve-hundred-pound animal to go into a tiny box on wheels.

People have to understand that a horse has good reason for feeling uncomfortable in small spaces. First, she's a lot bigger than a person. A space that feels roomy to us might not feel that way to a horse. Many people are so into their own thoughts and feelings that they can't imagine what a situation might be like for a horse.

Other situations that can induce feelings of claustrophobia in a horse include when a number of people or other horses crowd around her. Being put into a small stall or being led through a narrow hallway can also make a horse feel uncomfortable.

Again, like people, one horse might react differently than another to the same situation. Pawing, sweating, jogging sideways, trembling, heavy breathing, pinned ears, balking, and even pulling back, bucking, or rearing can all be signs that your horse feels claustrophobic.

Lisa, my co-author, has told me of a particular yearling. Years ago she was teaching him to load into a trailer. He was resistant, but finally one day after lots of consistency and patience, the colt jumped in. But then he became claustrophobic and froze in place, refusing to back out. He exhibited sweating and trembling, and certainly felt the walls of the trailer closing in on him. He was in there for a full two days, during which Lisa of course fed and watered him and spent time with him to try to ease his anxiety. She even brought his best buddy up to the outside of the trailer, thinking another horse could better convey how to get out than she could. Then after the forty-eight-hour mark had passed, the horse trusted her (and himself) enough to unload, and while he loaded and hauled throughout his life, he was never comfortable in any part of the process.

Trailering aside, if you have a horse who is claustrophobic, stay calm. There's nothing worse than a person having a conniption fit while her horse is having an emotional meltdown. Nothing good will come of that, I assure you. Focus on your horse and be patient.

Remember that your horse is frightened and uncomfortable, so you have to provide the exact same emotional support you would need in the same situation. Other than a cup of hot cocoa slathered with whipped cream and a pile of chunky chocolate chip cookies, I absolutely would want a calm, steadying presence that I could focus on to feel safe.

With a claustrophobic horse, whenever possible, give him space. Darcy is a volunteer leader and sidewalker at a local therapeutic riding program. She tells me that these programs know all about claustrophobic horses. When a horse has a rider, a leader, a nearby instructor, and (in some cases) two sidewalkers who walk alongside the rider and sometimes lean on the horse (although I am told that is definitely not good form), many horses become claustrophobic. That is a lot of people inside the horse's personal space. Darcy says some therapy horses can only tolerate one sidewalker, and others none at all. Every person's and every horse's personal space comes with slightly different boundaries.

Can a horse become less claustrophobic over time? Sometimes. I start by exposing any claustrophobic horse to a space, such as a large stall, and gradually decrease the size of the space over time. Or, I lead the horse by myself, and when he is comfortable, have someone else walk alongside him on the right side, near where a saddle would be. If the horse shows signs of discomfort, I have the person move away, and then gradually move closer again. I always pay attention to the horse's mood and body language. Hopefully, with time and patience, the horse will slowly become accustomed to smaller spaces and having a second person close by when being led.

When it comes to trailering, I paint the inside of my trailers a light color. Any interior designer, or a talented neighbor like I have in my friend Carole Carson, will tell you that light-colored walls make spaces look bigger. I prefer a light gray or pale green or blue to a white, though, because if light is shining inside the trailer, whites can look blindingly white and make vision impossible. This can truly convince your horse that going inside that tiny trailer is not a good idea—even if the rig is a nine-horse semi.

But here's my best advice on this: if your horse doesn't like crowds, or has difficulty going into tight or dark spaces, think of the situation from your horse's perspective. Remember that lights can look lighter and brighter to a horse than a human, and darks can look like a cosmic void. You can also put your eyes at your horse's eye height and take a look around. From there, you can begin to problem solve. What is it, specifically, that makes your horse nervous, and how can you change that specific detail to something that makes your horse feel safe? Trial and error will rule the day for a while, but hopefully you will hit on a thing, or a combination of things, that help.

Know, however, that like some people, some horses are always going to be uneasy in tight spaces.

HORSES DO NOT LOOK UPON EMOTIONAL PEOPLE AS SAFE AND COMPETENT LEADERS.

Sally Blue's owner, Agnes Temple, is a larger-than-life emotional roller coaster and is exhausting to be around. She can go from laughter to tears to enthusiasm to anxiety in the blink of an eye. And even

Tessie trusts that her competent leader will keep her safe from the "killer" umbrella.

though I love her dearly, would I follow her to safety during the zombie apocalypse? No, and neither would any of my horses.

We all know at least one person like Agnes. They are wonderful, but not people I would trust with my life. Horses feel the same, but because horses are prey animals, they have to quickly decide who will save them from the zombies, and who will lead them deeper into the fray. When a horse senses that a person is feeling emotional, it can make the horse feel threatened—and unsafe.

In addition, horses are creatures of habit, <u>and</u> they like to know what to expect. That's why consistency in training works. When someone is emotional, his or her behavior can be unpredictable, and that, too, can make a horse feel anxious and unsafe.

My foster son, Bubba, came to me when he was eleven, and anyone who has ever been around an eleven-year-old boy knows how loud and unpredictable their voices and movements can be. He loves horses, though, and couldn't understand why some of them did not love him back. Once I explained that he had to chill out, be quieter, more consistent, and more predictable, the leery horses finally started to engage with him.

Something we humans often do not think about, but that a horse always thinks of, is what an emotional person smells like. People put out all kinds of unique, weird, and funky smells when stressed or emotional, and while other humans sometimes don't pick up on that, a horse definitely will. The horse then comes to associate that kind of smell with unpredictable people, and an unsafe situation.

But here's the good news: no matter what kind of a roller coaster day, or week, or year (or life) you've had, you can change your relationship with your horse and become the calm, confident leader he or she needs.

This is what I do, because, holy cow, stumbling over a murder victim a few times a year can really get my emotions going. If I am around a horse and start to feel emotional, I clear my thoughts and feelings so I can concentrate only on my equine companion. All the surrounding noise of the farm gets weeded out of my brain. All my problems are shunted to a holding box inside my head, and my horse becomes the only thing I'm aware of. Then I give myself a pep talk. "Be confident. Be calm. Speak in a soft, firm voice. Avoid making loud noises or sudden movements."

Finally, I work to become fully aware of my body. A horse's safety depends on her being able to read human body language, so I take care to move quietly, confidently—and kindly. Honestly, this can take some months of practice, so don't give up if you feel frustrated at first. The effort is more than worth it, and your horse will really appreciate it.

A HORSE BEHAVES TOWARD YOU, LIKE YOU BEHAVE TOWARD HIM.
Simply put, if you act silly toward a horse, a horse will act silly toward you. Horses are masters at mirroring your thoughts and emotions—almost before you yourself know what they are, which is why they excel in therapeutic settings.

But horses are individuals, and can react differently to different people. Gigi is a young mare who loves life and loves to be silly. When I am around her, if I am unfocused, or laughing while talking with a friend, Gigi becomes more and more exuberant. But if I am quiet and focused, she settles down and focuses on me—as much as Gigi ever settles down and focuses. She rarely settles down around Bubba, because he rarely settles himself.

It isn't always in the moment that a horse replays your behavior, though. Past human behavior can have a lasting effect. I don't want to believe that people can be cruel or belligerent toward a horse, or any living thing, but I'd be naïve to think that kind of behavior doesn't exist. I've seen a lot of people who treat a horse as a tool, rather than a valued partner and companion. Whenever I encounter a horse who is aggressive, who pins his ears and makes ugly faces at me, I think that this is a horse who people have repeatedly been mean to, and so, he is being mean back.

Past negative behavior by people toward a horse can last a long, long time, and recovery from that will only happen on the horse's time frame, not yours. My co-author worked with a therapeutic riding horse who in a previous life had been a second-level Dressage horse. But, he pinned his ears at everyone, and most of the volunteers at that riding center thought the horse was mean. Lisa did some digging and in tracing the horse back to many previous owners, found a rumor the horse had once been badly beaten by a man with a pitchfork.

It turned out that the horse was not being mean or aggressive; he was being protective of himself. That made all the difference in the world, and with that knowledge, volunteers (mostly unconsciously, probably) changed their behavior toward him. Rather than being protective of themselves—because who wouldn't be when working around a horse who continuously had his ears back and made thrusting gestures with his chin—they became nurturing. Whenever he made mean faces, they just calmly said, "It's okay; you're okay," and continued grooming or whatever they were doing. The horse never fully recovered, but Lisa said he improved by about a thousand percent, all because the behavior of the people around him changed, and as a prey animal, he changed along with them to match their new, caring behavior.

I like Lisa's example, because horses, over time, can learn to anticipate certain behaviors from people, or from a specific person. Once the interactions consistently change, the horse's behavior should change, too. But remember, you can't place a time expectation on a horse when it comes to a behavior change—or anything else. Learning something new, whether it is how to trot over a pole, or exhibiting better manners, might take two to three days for one horse, and six to eight months for another.

WHEN A HORSE SUDDENLY BLOWS A BLAST OF AIR THROUGH HIS NOSE, HE'S CLEARING HIS NASAL PASSAGES SO HE CAN BREATHE IN NEW SCENT AND ASSESS HIS SAFETY.
I have to say, Bubba thinks this little fact is fascinating. And really, it is. A horse's nasal passages go way up toward his eyes, so there is

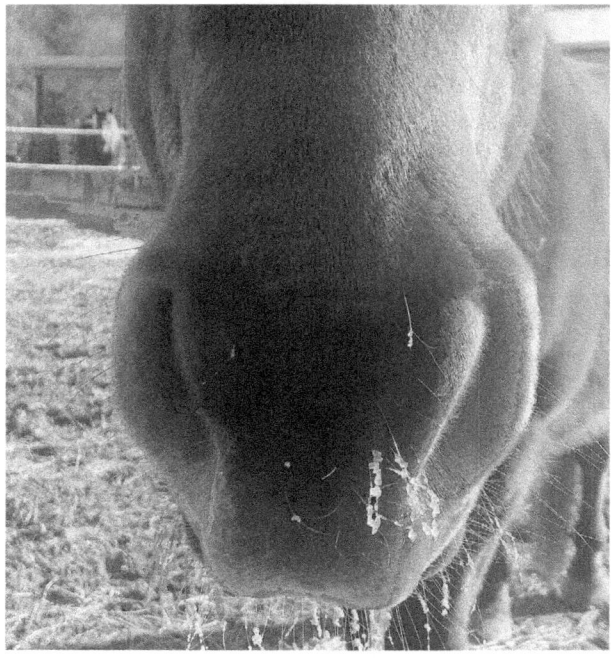

Cold temps can affect how or what your horse can smell.

a lot of space for scent to linger. Because horses are prey animals, they use their senses more than we do, with smell/scent being one of them. So, when a horse encounters a potentially dangerous situation, such as a stranger walking around the corner of the barn, a plastic bag blowing in the wind, or the wind itself blowing in unusual scent from up the road, a horse may blow all the air out of his nose in a huge snort, and then breathe in the unfamiliar scent.

Bubba likes to try this blowing technique sometimes himself, and actually, it's not a bad idea. The more we can learn to experience the world the way a horse does, the better we can understand and communicate with them.

A horse snorts for a variety of other reasons, too, not just to assess scent. Their noses are sensitive, and they can easily breathe dirt, dust, or other debris into their nasal passages. Snorting helps clear debris out of their nose so they can breathe more easily.

A gentler snort might happen when a horse is excited, such as when going down the trail. Snorting is a way to release his excitement and to signal to other horses (and humans) that he is happy.

Horses also snort to communicate with other horses. He might snort to let other horses know where he is, to warn others of danger, or to just say hi. Seeing a horse snort is usually a good thing, but if your horse snorts excessively, or in a way that seems to be causing pain, then by all means, consult your veterinarian.

JUST AS WITH PEOPLE, YOUR FACIAL EXPRESSION ALONE MAY BE ENOUGH TO DRIVE YOUR HORSE AWAY FROM YOU, OR INVITE HIM TO YOU.

Most horses spend a good portion of their lives studying human expression. It's a survival tactic, since horses use human expressions to help them understand our emotions and intentions.

I don't like to talk poorly about people, especially if they're not standing next to me where they can hear me call them on their crap. But, my neighbor two doors down, Hill Henley, is not a nice man. In fact, I've called him a slimy piece of trash, and that was when I was being nice. Unfortunately, he is my foster son's bio dad, and before he went to prison, he trained Tennessee Walking Horses. I only went over there a few times before Bubba came to live with me, but the horses in his barn were not happy horses.

I remember one horse in particular, a massive black mare who pinned her ears and aggressively stuck her chin out at me whenever I walked by her stall. But when I stopped and smiled at her, she looked at me as if I was from a different planet. It had probably been a long, long time since she had seen a friendly smile on a human face, so long that she was trying to remember what it was.

Suffice it to say that this mare understood an angry expression, since that was about all Hill ever had on his face. She associated the angry face with unpleasantness and with unpleasant humans, and obviously expected that from me. But my smile made her stop and pause, and I'd like to think if she had been in a barn where people were kind to her, and smiled more, then her ugly faces would not show up whenever a human walked past her stall.

The thing is, a horse can tell when you feel happy, sad, angry, or scared—often before you know those feelings yourself. There are a few reasons why a horse is so good at recognizing human facial expressions. First, they have excellent eyesight. Second, horses have a large brain for their size, which allows them to process information quickly and make decisions based on what they see. Third, horses have evolved to live in herds. That means they've had to learn how to communicate with each other as a survival skill. Facial expressions are one way that horses communicate with each other, so it's natural that they use the same method to communicate with us.

The horse's ability to recognize human facial expressions is important for both horses and humans. For horses, it helps them stay safe and interact with us in a positive way. For humans, it helps us build a better relationship with our horse and understand his needs.

I often tell my students to default to a pleasant but neutral expression when they work with their horse. They might frown when a horse makes a mistake, or use a big smile when their horse does something especially delightful. Opening their eyes wide indicates surprise to us—and to our horses. These and other facial expressions can make a difference whether a horse wants to work with you or not, or if he will give you his best.

A HORSE'S SUCCESSES AND FAILURES ARE A GOOD REFLECTION OF HER HUMAN'S ABILITY.
A horse who likes and trusts her human partner is far more likely to be successful in whatever activity she is being asked to do. That's just common sense, because people, I think, are exactly the same. I

always try really hard for someone I like and trust, such as my neighbor, Carole Carson, versus someone I don't, such as Hill Henley.

Of course, there are many other factors that contribute to a horse's success or failure, including the horse's physical ability, personality, and education, but I really think it's you, your skill and knowledge, and the connection you have with your horse that makes the real difference.

Here are a few things I do to help ensure each of my horse's successes.

First, I get to know the horse's personality and temperament. Each is an individual, and each has a different personality and intellect. Ringo, for example, has what I call a big personality. For me to be successful with him I had to, through my voice and body, show him I was up to his level. That included staying focused on him and responding to what he was telling me. Through trial and error I learned that when he shook his head back and forth early in our workout, it meant he wanted more: more pressure, more speed, more collection and balance. Only then did he relax and do his job. However, if I had not spent the time to learn his body language, we would not have been as productive in the show pen as we were.

I will shut up about Hill Henley soon, I promise, but he is the kind of man who thinks he knows everything about everything. Don't we all know at least one person like that? With horses, though, it's important that we learn every second we spend with them. It's been my experience that every time I look at a horse I learn something about him, myself, or life in general. I just have to be open to it.

So this is my challenge to you: keep learning. Try a discipline that is different from your area of expertise. If you ride Dressage, take a barrel racing lesson. Watch a video from a trainer you have just learned about. Try a new riding technique, or take time to watch your horse interact in the herd. Every single day you will learn something important, and your horse skills, connection, and success will only continue to grow.

HORSES USE THEIR ENTIRE BODY TO COMMUNICATE.

I think if I was a horse I'd be so frustrated with people. Every day, all day, horses use their bodies to communicate with us and we ignore 90 percent (or more) of that communication. How frustrating that must be, especially when it is our job as lovers of horses to understand their language.

Spike communicates his displeasure to Quincy by pinning his ears, and swinging his head and neck in Quincy's direction.

A while back I taught my neighbor, hunky country music mega-star Keith Carson, to ride for a music video he was doing. The entire process was far more challenging than I had planned. Mostly because I have this not-so-secret crush on the man and live for the days he washes his boat in his driveway near the bushes that separate our properties. Might I add that usually he is only wearing his swim trunks? On those days I have been known to get a sudden urge to get the hedge clippers and spend a great deal of time carefully trimming said bushes. It . . . okay, my co-author tells me I'm getting off track. She's right.

My point is that teaching Keith to ride was also more difficult than I expected, because at first, he didn't understand the concept of equine body language. He wanted to be a "get on and go" kind of a rider. But it doesn't work that way.

Riding is a partnership, and you and your horse are partners. Your horse has thoughts and feelings and opinions, and communicates all of that to you, continuously. If you are to be in a successful partnership with your horse, you must learn to pay attention to all of that—and to respond accordingly.

My mother had cancer and died before I was ten. One of the few things I remember about her was that when I spoke to her, she often did not respond and I spent most of my time when I was eight and nine years old being quite frustrated with her. Of course, I didn't understand that, mostly, she was too sick to respond, or that she often was sleeping.

It was quite good that after a few unproductive days of trying to ride, Keith finally understood when I mentioned, again, that when our trusty aged gelding, Bob, swished his tail like that, he was not swishing at flies. He was telling Keith that he was using too much leg pressure, and was asking him too forcefully. Bob was telling Keith to back off, and finally, Keith understood. After that, Keith and Bob got along great, and Keith started to ask what every little body movement meant. I love when a student makes that connection, because only then can they truly become a rider.

Horses, of course, don't just use their bodies to communicate with us, they use body language to communicate likes, dislikes, fears, and safety issues with their equine friends, too. One of the most common ways horses communicate is with their ears. A horse can move his ears independently of each other, and through this, can communicate a variety of emotions. For example, a horse with his ears pinned back is feeling either threatened or aggressive, while a horse with his ears pointed forward is curious or interested. Sideways ears can mean confusion or discomfort. In general, though, wherever a horse's ears are pointed, that's what he is thinking about.

Eye contact is another way horses communicate. Horses make eye contact with each other to communicate dominance or submission. A horse who makes direct eye contact with another horse is asserting dominance, while a horse who avoids eye contact is submissive.

A horse also uses his tail to communicate a variety of emotions, including fear, aggression, and excitement. For example, a horse who feels afraid, or who is experiencing anxiety or pain can swish his tail back and forth. A horse who is feeling excited will often raise his tail. And, an up and down flapping movement of the tail can indicate annoyance. Sometimes, though, all the swishing and flapping can just mean your horse is using his tail as a fly swatter.

We have to remember, too, that horses use a variety of sounds to communicate with each other, including whinnies, nickers, and snorts. Whinnies are often used to greet other horses or to call for attention. Sally Blue rarely whinnies, except when someone comes to get her from the pasture to go into the barn before dinner. Then she whinnies, loudly, the first instant she sees someone coming to get her.

I think she's saying, "It's about time you got here!"

But Agnes Temple, her owner, says, "No, dear. Sally is trying to place her dinner order and really, she'd much rather have sliced apples and carrots with some mints thrown in than her grain and supplements. Now really, dear, why can't she have that?"

Other than the fact that a steady diet of apples and carrots could cause Cushing's, a sort of equine diabetes, no, there's nothing wrong with that. But back to the subject matter at hand.

Nickers, those soft, low, "huh, huh, huh" sounds that a horse makes are very different from loud whinnies. Nickers express affection, a polite ask, or are used to greet someone familiar.

We've already talked about snorts so I won't repeat myself here. But, understanding what a horse is trying to communicate means humans have to put all of this together, along with the situation a horse is in. If Sally has her head raised, is taking short strides, and is blowing through her nose when we are out on the trail and it's windy, well, she might be having trouble figuring out where a specific smell is coming from because she thinks the wind is blowing scent around like a kite in a tornado. Actually, it might just be a little breezy. Sally sometimes gets a teensy bit dramatic about wind.

Anyway, that is a completely different scenario from when we are in the outdoor arena, and Sally has her head lowered, and is walking out with nice long strides and snorting. In the first scenario, she is unsure, in the second, she is just feeling good. You have to look at the entire horse, and the horse's surroundings, before you make a decision about what your horse is saying, and more important, how to react to the communication.

A HORSE SLEEPS LESS THAN THREE HOURS A DAY, MOSTLY IN FIFTEEN- TO TWENTY-MINUTE BURSTS.
I love sleeping. In a way, it's like teleporting yourself to breakfast and to that first, delicious cup of coffee, or for me, hot chocolate.

People tend to need a lot of sleep, but it's a different story when it comes to horses. While various research studies differ (mildly) about the number of hours of sleep a horse needs, all agree that it's not very much. A Kentucky Equine Research study found that a horse will spend five to seven hours a day in "resting behavior," but only needs about thirty minutes of deep, lying down kind of sleep. Often, the sleep is broken into short naps, but if a horse doesn't get the chance to lie down and get those thirty minutes in, he can become sleep deprived. (Young horses are the exception, and like human babies, need more sleep.)

Many factors can affect how much sleep a horse gets, including their age, health, and environment. For example, a horse with a health problem may have trouble sleeping. Horses who are older

Lex, who is lower in the herd pecking order than Spike, often watches over Spike when he naps.

and arthritic, or horses who are very heavy may find lying down to get that deep sleep and then getting up difficult or painful, so they just don't. Providing deep bedding to create a soft space for them to lie can encourage these horses to get more rest.

And, a horse who is in a noisy or stressful environment, such as being stalled overnight at a horse show, may also have trouble sleeping. Then when you are ready to compete your horse is not at his best since he is exhausted.

As a competitive trainer, my horses are frequently stalled for several days to a week or more at one show or another. That's why I do my best to provide the following:

One is to not feed a big meal too close to bedtime. As with people, digestion can cause some horses to have trouble sleeping.

Another idea is to make the sleeping area as dark as possible. Remember that horses see much better in low light than we do, so bright lights can be especially annoying to some horses, as can the flicker of fluorescent lighting that is found in many show barns. At home, if your horses are stalled, keep the lights off at night. If you are at a horse show, some stall drapings may or may not reduce light into your horse's stall or provide an increased sense of safety and comfort. Partial stall drapings also can visually block the view into your horse's stall so if your horse gets cast or is not feeling well, human eyes may not spot this as early as without the drapings.

Finally, if your horse is not sleeping well, try a white noise machine or a fan. especially when you travel. If you can't reproduce lighting your horse is used to at home, coming close to reproducing the sounds your horse usually hears will help.

I never sleep well in a hotel the first night, because the sounds are so different from my little farm house at home. I can understand the same might apply to a horse. A white noise machine or a fan won't completely drown out unfamiliar sounds at a show, but it will mask some sounds, muffle others, and reduce the effects of the unfamiliar setting. Possibly, it will even allow your horse to lie down and get some needed sleep.

However, I have come to the conclusion that Gigi is never going to sleep at a show. In fact, I don't think she's had a wink of deep sleep since the day she was born. With Gigi, we've tried a lot of things that work well for other horses, but do not work for her. Sigh.

HORSES DEVELOPED AN INTUITIVE NATURE BECAUSE THEY ARE PREY ANIMALS.

Those of you who have read the mysteries about me that my co-author writes know that my horse Sally Blue may or may not be psychic. Looking back, she certainly did seem to give clues that solved some of the mysteries, but then again, is she just a very intuitive mare?

Because a horse is a prey animal, to survive she has to intuit the good, bad, irresponsible, and silly intention of every living thing within her proximity. As a result, horses have developed some pretty unique skills. In my opinion, people have lost much of that ability to intuit. I walked into a lunch meeting with the owner of one of my training horses some years ago. I was so focused on my plan to give him a good report on his horse, that I was blindsided by his intention to fire me. I intuited not one thing about his actions. Later, I felt as dumb as a thumb.

If I had been more horse-like, I would have sensed that he was not happy with my training methods, or my results. I hate it when I plan my day and other people don't follow the script. But I learned something, and that was to be more aware of other people, what they might be thinking, and how they might act in a given situation.

Horses are so good at this. They look at a person (or a dog or a bird or a snake) and instinctively sense what it's going to do. This is where the mindset of a prey animal kicks in, because always, they look for danger and a way to escape. It's a good thing horses can run so fast. Because they can easily out-run most predators, that has become their go-to method of finding safety. They intuit, react, and find safety as needed.

In addition to using vision to intuit intent, a horse can also smell a person or predator's intent from a long way away, which gives them even more time to escape. This is one reason the herd is so important to a horse. When one horse deciphers bad intent, the entire herd can protect itself by running for safety. In this way, horses work together to defend themselves. If only we people worked together nearly as well.

FLUORESCENT LIGHTS, SUCH AS THOSE OFTEN FOUND IN THE BARNS OF SHOW FACILITIES, CAN QUICKLY TIRE A HORSE'S EYES AND BRAIN.
We've talked about how horses see differently than people, but to take it one more step, a horse's brain reacts differently to light than ours does. For example, a horse is more sensitive to blue and yellow light than to red light, obviously because they don't have the cone that allows them to see reds.

But. this means a horse can see fluorescent lights better than we can. Fluorescent lights emit a very narrow band of light, which is why they sometimes appear to flicker. This flickering can be jarring to horses, and can make them feel anxious or uncomfortable. If you use fluorescent lights around horses, try to see that they are shielded, so the light does not shine directly into the horse's eyes.

When I asked our veterinarian about this, he said that horses have a reflective layer of tissue behind the retina in their eye. This layer helps reflect light back through the retina, which improves night vision. But it also makes fluorescent lights appear brighter and more intense to horses. Therein lies the problem.

If you have a choice at home, try incandescent or LED lights, which are less likely to flicker. We have LED lights and like them in our barn here at Cat Enright Stables, but when we travel to a show, we have no choice in the lighting in the barn where the horses are stalled. And often, the lights are turned on most of the night. I have lobbied, somewhat successfully, at shows to implement a "lights-out" time from an hour after the last class to two hours before the first class. Horses need their rest!

A HORSE BECOMES A HERD WITH ANY PERSON WHO INTERACTS WITH HER.

One of my pet peeves is when a horse misbehaves, and the person calls the horse stupid, or stubborn. Really, all the horse is doing is letting you know he is in pain, or he is testing boundaries for herd leadership, because in the mind of the horse, you and he are a herd. When the horse tests, and tries to find out who in your little herd of two is the leader, many people don't take time to figure out the behavior. It's a simple concept, but sometimes I feel someone left the bag of idiots open. I don't mean to offend, but I tell it like I see it. When something as important as this is the topic of discussion, it physically hurts to hold in my thoughts—so I don't.

We've already determined that horses are prey animals, and have an instinctual need to be in a herd. Safety in numbers and all that. When a horse is around a human, he tries to determine if the human is a leader or a follower. If the horse perceives the human to

Quincy doesn't like to make decisions on his own, so he accepts most people as his leader, even kids who just want to love him.

be a leader, he will more likely be cooperative. However, if the horse perceives the human to be a follower, he may start to misbehave to assert his dominance. After all, even in a herd of two, someone has to be in charge. The horse really doesn't want the leadership role, but if the human doesn't show any more leadership than wallpaper paste, then the horse will think, "I'll just have to step up and take charge. One of us has to keep us both safe."

There are a several ways a horse can behave when testing a human for leadership. Some common behaviors can include refusing to move forward, bucking, kicking, biting, pinning his ears, and swishing his tail. If a horse tests you for leadership, establish yourself as the leader by using clear and consistent commands, and project an air of confidence. But remember, a horse can see inside your soul and knows you better than you know yourself. It has to be true confidence or the horse will know you are a poser.

There are some horses, like our gelding Bob, who are calm, confident and forgiving horses. They don't test for leadership much, and accept that most humans will keep them safe. They can, however, show signs of agitation or tension if they are entrusted to someone who they think popped out of the idiot bag. Raised head, wide eyes, swishing tail and the like are all good indicators that a horse thinks his human is lacking in good sense.

To become a strong herd leader with your horse, remember that trust and respect can take time—and it's all on the horse's time frame, not yours. You'll get there quicker if you interact with him with consistency, fairness, and if you reward good behavior, rather than punish bad manners.

HORSES WHO ARE OUT ON PASTURE CAN GRAZE TWELVE OR MORE HOURS A DAY.
Actually, the *Journal of Equine Veterinary Science* reported that a horse will graze ten to seventeen hours a day, with the eating broken into fifteen to twenty grazing periods.

Wouldn't it be great if we were hard-wired to eat that many hours a day? I'd choose fields of chocolate and strawberries, pepperoni pizza, and chunky mint chocolate chip ice cream. Not sure that I'd like more than a dozen hours of eating grass, but horses do. Horses also have a complex digestive system that's designed to break down cellulose, which is the main component of grass. Their small stomach and long intestine allow them to digest large amounts of forage slowly. They also have a special organ called the cecum, which is where cellulose is broken down by bacteria.

On a side note, have you heard of the cecal swing? If you look at a horse head on, sometimes the right side of the horse (which would be your left if you are looking at him from the front) is larger than the left side. This is what I call the cecal swing and it's caused by the horse digesting cellulose in the cecum. Some horses always have a bit of a cecal swing, others not so much. Some horses have a huge cecal swing, and this can make it difficult to ride a balanced seat, since it causes a rider's left leg to lie straight down alongside the horse's barrel, but then the rider's right leg has to cant outward from the hip to curve around the cecal swing. Since the rider is then not symmetrically balanced left and right, it makes for a more difficult ride. It can also make fitting a saddle a nightmare, but that is a topic for later in the book.

Given the option to graze on pasture, the amount of time a horse spends eating (and ingesting all that grass that keeps the cecum busy) varies. This is due to many factors, including the quality of forage, the weather, and the horse's level of activity. Horses who are turned out on <u>pasture</u> usually spend more time grazing than horses in stalls do eating hay. Horses who are working or exercising heavily may also need to eat more—and more often.

I understand it's not always possible to turn your horse out on pasture for many hours a day, which is what most horses need. But if you can, do it. Some horses have health issues, such as insulin resistance or Cushing's disease that prevents this. Too much fresh grass, especially in the spring when the grass is lush, can cause laminitis, which can be lethal to horses. Laminitis, by the way, is the inflammation of sensitive layers of tissue called the laminae that is inside the hoof. And if you're thinking, "My goodness, horses are fragile creatures," yes, you would be correct.

If you board and don't have long periods of turn out, or if your horse has to be stalled due to an injury, or maybe your horse is at a big, week-long show, do the best you can by providing a variety of hay and forage to keep your horse's mind busy and his digestive system happy.

These four horses are each <u>facing</u> a different direction, watching for predators and keeping each other safe as they graze.

A BAD ATTITUDE IS THE FIRST SIGN A HORSE IS HURTING.
Most horses want to be kind and helpful. If they aren't, there often is pain involved. Hillbilly Bob is usually placid and focused, a guy who knows his job in and out of the show pen. Last year, however, he pinned his ears when Bubba got on. He moved off at a walk okay,

but after the ride started, he began to pin his ears again. Further inspection revealed a slight swelling along his right rib cage that Bubba had not noticed when he saddled Bob. During that time frame, we had been turning Bob out with bouncy Gigi. While we will never know what happened, she probably kicked him while trying to engage him in play. Gigi lives to play. The take away is that your horse wants to please you. If he or she is unwilling, be creative about finding the source of the unwillingness. Most often that will be pain, but it can take some trial and error, and possibly the services of a veterinarian, chiropractor, acupuncturist, farrier, or other professional to solve the problem.

Also, because horses are prey, they have a natural instinct to hide pain, because showing pain can make them more vulnerable to predators. As a result, a horse may try to mask pain by acting normal. However, if the pain is too severe, your horse may start to show signs of discomfort, such as a bad attitude.

We used to have a horse in the barn named Reddy. She was a true diva, and unlike many horses, wore her every feeling in the expression on her face. When she was not 100 percent, she might buck, kick, or snap at her human. She'd go on hunger strikes and listlessly come out of her stall only when asked firmly. All of these behaviors indicate something is wrong, but with Reddy it could be something as simple as mosquito bites—although I admit they can be as annoying as washing bird doo doo off your windshield. With other horses, though, it could be something quite serious.

If you notice any of these signs, think creatively to solve the problem. Or better yet, call your vet.

THE HORSE HERD IS MATRIARCHAL, WITH A LEAD MARE (A MARE WITH A STRONG PERSONALITY) WHO CONTROLS THE MOVEMENT, SAFETY, AND ETIQUETTE OF THE HERD.
In the wild, horses usually live in groups of related females and their offspring. The herd is led by a matriarch, who is usually one of the oldest and/or most experienced females in the herd. The matriarch is responsible for leading the herd to food and water, and also helps protect the herd from predators. She also watches over others as they sleep.

Veterinarian Joe Bertone, DVM, MS, DACVIM, has documented more than one hundred sleep deprived horses during his career. He says that many horses need a strong female presence in the herd to feel comfortable enough to sleep. Mares are responsible for the day-to-day well-being of the herd and act as sentinels who watch over other horses as they rest.

He also says that males can fill the role, but in general, it is a mare's job. There have been studies that show horses will look to the nearest mare before lying down, probably because they feel safer knowing a mare is on lookout. They don't seem to trust geldings or stallions as much. In fact, according to Bertone, the practice of separating mares and geldings into different fields may lead to very tired boys.

Lisa currently has a very strong matriarch in her herd. Tessie, whom you have seen photos of here, checks every new visitor to the farm out by looking them in the eye, and then up and down. She might as well be the Queen of England vetting you and deciding if you are worth talking to. Only after Tessie has dropped her head in a definite sign of approval, can the rest of the herd approach a newcomer.

Tessie also is the one who decides when the herd goes to get water, when they go out to the pasture to eat, and when they come back to the run-in sheds. All of this might seem a bit much, but it's a way to keep the herd safe. Lisa says if you watch Tessie's herd closely, you can see the communication between the horses, the ask to go to the water trough, and the nod to go ahead.

This is most likely true of your herd as well, so take time to watch the body language and the dynamics. Know, too, that if your horse is turned out in a paddock by himself, he is still a herd with horses in other visible paddocks. Watch closely. You will be amazed.

A HORSE HEARS THINGS THAT A HUMAN PHYSICALLY CAN'T.
This is another area we often overlook when troubleshooting equine behavior. A horse's senses are so much greater than ours. So much so that when you think your horse is spooking at nothing, possibly your horse is hearing something you can't.

While the results of research studies on the matter vary somewhat, numerous studies have found that some horses can hear sounds up to two miles away. Why, you ask, the better hearing? One reason is that a horse's very life depends on being able to hear a predator approach. Another reason is that her large ears can swivel most any direction to better hear a predator. A horse also needs great hearing to find mates, establish social bonds, and follow the rules of the herd. So if she can't hear, or can't hear well, all of that might be compromised.

A horse also has a wider range of hearing than a human. Louisiana State University has reported that while a human can hear in ranges from 64 hertz (Hz) to 23,500 Hz, a horse can hear in the ranges of 55 Hz to 33,500 Hz. Other studies report different, but very similar, ranges for both horses and for humans. This means in general, a horse hears sounds in higher and lower registers than a human can.

Lex certainly has some big listening ears!

A hertz, by the way, measures the number of wave cycles (or sound frequencies) that pass through a given point in a single second. One hertz is equal to one cycle per second, so one hertz is equal to sixty vibrations per minute.

Hearing in horses can also deteriorate with age. A study from the University of Queensland in Australia found that many older horses experience a mild to moderate hearing loss. Their testing was done with two groups of horses. One group had horses between the ages of five and eight, and the other had horses between the ages of seventeen and twenty-two. Just as with many older people, they found that many of the older horses showed a significant hearing loss. So maybe your horse didn't spook at something she usually does, because she didn't hear the sound that accompanies the object. A barking dog, for example, the crash of a tree branch, or the whoosh of a car when it passed on the road.

The bottom line is that when it comes to sound vibrations, horses can actually hear, for example, the ultrasonic call of a bat. Bubba tells me that this is his one true wish, to hear ultrasonic bat calls. While that would be cool, if we are talking about wishes, I'm thinking more along the lines of a warm beach with lots of sand and sun. And no bats.

IF A HORSE DOES NOT FOLLOW THE SOCIETAL RULES OF THE HERD, THE HERD LEADER WILL BANISH THE HORSE FROM ANY INTERACTION WITH THE OTHER HORSES.

We already know that horses are social animals. And, we also know that the herd leader is responsible for keeping the herd safe. But the herd leader also makes sure that everyone follows the rules. If a horse does not get with the program, so to speak, the herd leader might just banish the horse from the herd. This is a serious punishment because it means the horse will be on his own and will be more vulnerable to predators.

There are a few reasons why a horse might be banished. One reason is if the horse is aggressive and is a danger to the other horses. Another reason is if the horse is sick or injured and is a drain on the resources of the herd. Finally, a horse might be banished if he doesn't follow the rules or isn't contributing to the herd in a meaningful way. For example, a horse who doesn't help defend the herd or who doesn't help find food and water might be banished. As you might imagine, being banished can be a lonely and stressful experience.

Colby's Army once had a bright chestnut off-track Thoroughbred gelding who was frequently banished from their herd. The other horses would all be grazing together while this horse <u>stood</u> in a far corner. Each time he tried to approach the other horses Tessie ran him off. This continued for two or three days at a stretch. Then he'd be part of the herd for a week or so before he was once again banished.

In tracing the horse's history, Lisa found he had come from a small farm and had never gotten to be part of a real herd before he was shipped off to the track. Because of that, this horse didn't know how to behave around other horses and frequently committed socially unacceptable acts. Eventually he learned, but it took him the better part of a year.

If you are ever around a herd of horses, I hope you will take time to watch them interact with each other. With a better understanding of the herd comes a better understanding of the horse—and of you in relation to horses.

PEOPLE EXPECT RESPECT. WITH HORSES, YOU HAVE TO EARN IT. A few months ago, I interviewed a recent college graduate for a position as a barn helper. The position was open because, as I noted earlier, Jon Gardner, my barn manager, assistant trainer, right hand, and possible boyfriend is taking a break. Actually, I'm not sure exactly where he is, although he does check in with Bubba every week or so. As my dad's girlfriend, Marissa, once said to me, "Cat, there are plenty of fish in the sea. You just happen to suck at fishing." And people wonder why we are not close. Again, I digress.

Because Jon is gone, the job I was hiring for was full time cleaning stalls and tack, turning out horses, feeding, and the like. For the right person it could have turned into an assistant trainer position. I liked this particular candidate very much, but when it came time to talk money, she insisted on sixty-three thousand dollars a year. I don't know about where you live, but in middle Tennessee, I don't know any farm that pays that for barn help— especially for someone who has never held a job before. When it came to the job, this candidate had a lot of horse show experience and great grades, but zero experience as an employee. Zero. I wasn't willing to take the risk for that kind of salary.

What got me most, however, was that she kept insisting she was worth the money, that she was deserving of it. Really? If I had been a lead mare, I would have kicked her deserving entitlement across the pasture. When it comes to jobs (and pretty much everything else), I vote that we all become more like the horse herd and wait for others to earn their way to respect, rather than caving in when someone just expects it.

Lead mares don't lead because they want the job. They lead because they feel they could best keep the herd safe. Then they earn the respect the job entails by showing the other horses they are consistent, reliable, and show sound judgment. This doesn't always come overnight, either. It can come over time, over many months or years. Only then will the other horses allow the lead mare to lead.

We can't expect a prey animal like a horse to think like a predator (meaning like a human). For you to build a trusting, meaningful, and respectful relationship with your horse, you need to do the same things a lead mare would do.

Calm, consistent confidence goes a long way toward teaching a horse that you are deserving of her respect, and toward overriding her inherent need to flee unusual situations. Patience is also helpful. I remember when I was first starting out and I very busily and purposefully set goals for each horse's learning. I expected that by the third ride, for example, a horse would be steering and stopping well. Imagine my surprise when some horses didn't learn that fast. Maybe I didn't know everything after all. It was an eye-opening lesson that in everything we do with horses we operate on the horse's time frame for learning, and not on ours.

I also learned I had to show the same calm, consistent confidence with a slow learner that I did with a faster learner, and that I couldn't ever show my frustration. Ever. I needed to earn the leadership role in the relationship between the horse and myself. If I just expected the horse to respect me, that respect would never come. It was a good lesson for a young trainer, and one I will never forget.

SOME TRAINERS STUDY THE WHORLS ON A HORSE'S FOREHEAD. When I was in college a major colt-starting competition was held at our arena. I watched, fascinated, as the cowboys (for that year they were, truly, all cowboys), chose the colts they were going to work with over the next few days.

Some walked into the milling group of three-year-old geldings, who other than basic medical care, had never been handled. The cowboys waved their hats at the horses and watched, or they crouched down and called to a specific horse. But one cowboy simply looked at their faces, head-on if he could.

I asked one of my professors what he was doing and she said he was looking at the whorls, the cowlicks each horse has on his

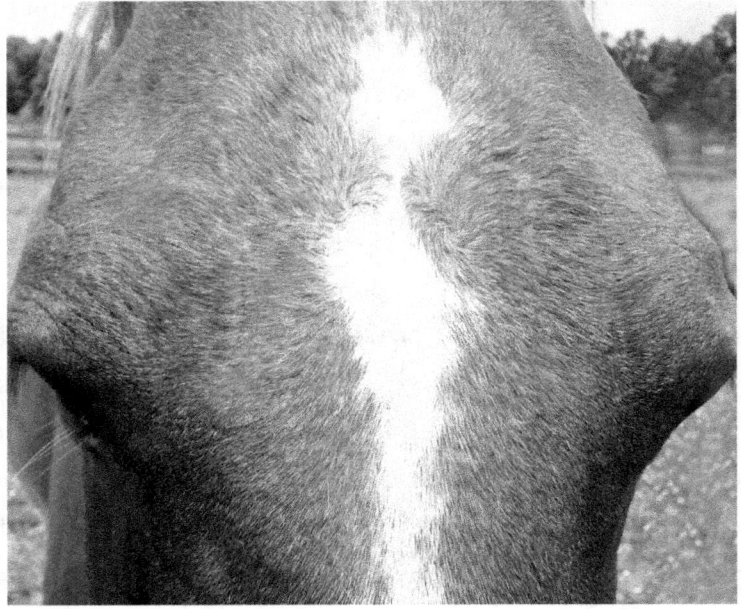

Tessie's double whorls on her forehead indicate she may have a strong personality. And yes, she does!

forehead between his eyes. That was my first introduction to the study of whorl patterns, and I have remained fascinated ever since. Many trainers have become experts on this, but if you choose one for more information, check out Linda Tellington-Jones. She was one of the first to tell the masses about this, and continues to do so very well.

Whorls can be found on just about any part of the horse's body, but they are most common on the face. And, they serve several purposes. Back in the day, cowboys used whorls to identify horses. Each horse's whorls are unique, so they can be used to single out horses who do not have any other markings. Think of a solid chestnut or a solid bay horse running in a herd of other mostly solid chestnut or bay horses. Look at the whorl on the forehead, and you will start to separate each horse out in your mind.

More important, whorls are thought to be related to a horse's personality. Some people believe that horses with certain whorl patterns are more intelligent, athletic, or gentle than others. I am one of these people, and we'll get to that in a minute.

Whorls are formed in the womb at about the same time a horse's personality forms. At least that's my understanding of it. It makes sense to me then, that a horse's forehead whorl and personality and drive could be connected.

Some also believe that the direction of a whorl can indicate a horse's handedness. Horses with whorls that point clockwise are usually right-handed, while a horse with a whorl that points counterclockwise are usually left-handed. I, personally, have found this to be true. Most of the time anyway.

While true experts can find meaning in whorls across a horse's body. I have only dived in as far as the forehead, but if you find this interesting, there is a lot of information out there on whorls on other parts of the horse's body.

On a side note, other than the direction of the swirl of a whorl, or cowlick, on a person's head possibly indicating whether a person is left- or right-handed, I have not found much information about whorls on people. I'd love to learn, though, since Bubba has a lot of cowlicks and is definitely a handful.

Back to equine forehead whorls. Here's what I know. A single whorl right between the eyes usually means a consistent, compliant, easy-going personality. I have worked with exceptions to this, but more often than not I have found this to be the case.

A single whorl above a horse's eyes can mean an active mind, while a whorl lower than the eyes indicates a less active mind. And, the more focused the whorl, the more possible focus in the mind, and vice versa.

Double whorls can indicate more complicated personalities. Horses with multiple forehead whorls can be more difficult to work with, and possibly, more inconsistent and unpredictable. Double whorls are most likely to be positioned as either side-by-side, or one on top of the other

But, many horses I have worked with who are highly-successful in national-level competition have high, side-by-side double whorls that are very close together. This kind of double whorl I think gives a horse the ability to focus exceptionally well. And, Darcy tells me that two of the most challenging therapy horses she has worked with have also been two of the best therapy horses, and both are side-by-side double whorl horses.

A double whorl with one on top of the other is tougher, because this can mean an extreme personality. It's like the double whorled side-by-side personality on steroids, and for my student population, I find these horses to be too untrustworthy to be recommended for purchase.

Note that a horse with multiple whorls that come together to look like the letter Z can be so unpredictable as to be dangerous. The two horses I have had who have been hard buckers, regular bolters, or who occasionally flipped themselves over backwards all had Z-shaped forehead whorls. Coincidence? Sally Blue says no.

And in case you're wondering, Sally Blue has double side-by-side whorls just above the eye. Hillbilly Bob has a single whorl below the eye. Darcy's Petey has a single whorl above the eye, and Gigi has side-by-side double whorls below the eye.

Take from this what you like. But seriously, if you have a horse, check out his or her forehead whorl(s) and see if your horse doesn't fall into the categories above.

Horse Care

I hope you found something of value in the previous section. Next, while we'll talk about horse care (because horses really are quite fragile) we're going to build on what we learned in the first section about horse behavior.

HORSES ON PASTURE SPEND ABOUT 60 PERCENT OF THEIR TIME GRAZING, WHILE STALLED HORSES SPEND ONLY 15 PERCENT OF THEIR TIME EATING—ONE REASON BEHAVIOR ISSUES DEVELOP MORE OFTEN WITH STALLED HORSES THAN PASTURED HORSES. My former boyfriend, the one before Jon, is a veterinarian. Probably, we'd still be together if his mother had one iota of graciousness in her being, but that's another story. He once gave me a book called *Equine Behavior: A Guide for Veterinarians and Equine Scientists* and we absolutely will not go into the fact that it was one of his former textbooks that he tried to pass off as a gift.

But in it, the text confirmed what most of us already know, that a pastured horse spends a lot of time eating, and stalled horses inhale their hay before you've even closed up the barn door. Then, once a stalled horse has no more to eat, he finds other ways to amuse himself. Sometimes that amusement includes poking a stick of hay up his nose, or lying down and rolling into the stall wall and becoming stuck.

Once, I showed up for the morning feed shift at the boarding barn I worked at when I was in high school to find a stalled horse with a huge gash on the side of his neck that was about a foot long. But after checking the stall, I found absolutely nothing, nothing at all, that the horse could have gotten hurt on. There was no hair attached to a splinter of wood, no blood in the shavings or in the stall, and the stall doors had been closed so a neighboring horse could not have reached over to bite him. How he got hurt badly enough to require a dozen stitches, I'll never know, but then again, I often think horses are on a lifelong mission to kill themselves.

Other than injuries, stalled horses also can develop destructive habits such as snapping at people and displaying a bad temperament. The horse could also start weaving (where the horse remains stationary but continually shifts his weight from one front leg to the other while swaying his head back and forth), pacing (either walking circles in the stall or repeatedly walking along one or two of the walls), or cribbing (grabbing a hard surface with his teeth, tightening his neck muscles and pulling back, often emitting a grunt. Overall, over time, it can badly damage the teeth).

The problem with stalls is that horses need space to move around. Lots of space. When they are confined to a twelve-foot by twelve-foot stall, they can become bored and restless, and that can lead to behavior problems. In addition, stalled horses have less social interaction. When isolated, they can become lonely and anxious, and that, too, can lead to negative behaviors.

I do understand that sometimes a stall is the only choice. Your horse may be recovering from an injury, or maybe the only boarding stable for miles and miles keeps their horses mostly stalled. If that's the case, give your horse as much turn-out time as possible and some friends to interact with.

At Cat Enright Stables, we do stall our horses sometimes. Recently we gutted our barn and put in the European-style of stalls where each horse can see all of the other horses and can put their heads out into the aisle. We also provide some of the horses toys to keep them occupied. Balls, treat dispensers, or slow-feeder hay nets can help, as can an in-stall friend, such as a goat—or even a chicken. Some horses even respond favorably and calm down when listening to classical music. Each horse is different, so some trial and error might be involved, but the main goal is to replace as much as possible the grazing, roaming, and social interaction the horse so desperately needs.

HAY, THE MAIN FOOD SOURCE FOR MOST HORSES, CONTAINS ABOUT 11 PERCENT WATER.
In the wild, horses intentionally pick and choose grasses with high water content to keep from getting dehydrated. Horses are smart, and their bodies are too, since they are very good at conserving water. While a horse can go a much longer period of time without drinking than a human can, she does need to get some water from her food.

When given the chance, a horse will do this by choosing grasses with high water content. The problem is that, for the most part, we have taken away the horse's ability to graze over miles and miles of land that offers a variety of grasses. Usually, a pasture will contain only one or two varieties of grass, and those might not be a kind that is high in water. On open range, a horse can pick and choose from a wide variety of grass, legumes, and even herbs.

In addition to grass, horses get water from other sources. These days that's usually a water trough or an automatic waterer. Sometimes it's a creek or pond. Regardless the source, I shouldn't have to say that the water needs to be checked regularly for cleanliness and hazards such as chemicals, so I won't mention that. At all.

Horses also usually don't care for water that is too hot or too cold and they can become dehydrated if the water is not between 45- and 65-degrees Fahrenheit. "Divas!" you might say, and in part, that's true, but keep in mind their bodies are different from ours, and they need what they need.

EVERY DAY, THE AVERAGE HORSE EATS A MINIMUM OF 1 PERCENT OF HIS BODY WEIGHT IN FORAGE (GRASS OR HAY), SO A 1,000-POUND HORSE WILL EAT TEN POUNDS OF HAY.
This is just a guideline; the amount of forage a horse needs will vary depending on his age, activity level, genetics, and overall health. For example, a growing horse or a horse who is working hard might need to eat several times more than a horse who is not as active.

Unfortunately for her, Sally Blue is what is called an "easy-keeper," meaning that she needs less hay (and grain) than average for her height, weight, breed, and temperament. Petey is on the other end of the spectrum. Even after keeping free-choice, high-quality hay in front of him at all times, and maxing out the amount of grain he should get, Petey always looks fit and trim.

It's been my experience that a draft horse, or a draft cross such as a Haflinger or Lisa's lead mare, Tessie, needs surprisingly little to maintain weight, to the point of having to add a ration balancer—a supplement filled with vitamins and minerals—to be sure they get all they need. Probably, a horse who is more energetic, such as an Arabian, Thoroughbred, or Saddlebred will need more grass or hay. However, there are exceptions to every rule.

Non-horse people always seem surprised at the amount of food a horse needs. A few weeks ago we got our monthly delivery

Lex's daily half-pound of grain includes a ration balancer.

of hay, two hundred bales at a cost of two thousand dollars. Agnes happened to be there and was so excited that we had our "yearly" delivery and that the hay barn was full. When I explained that was the amount of hay the ten horses in the barn would eat in a single month, she was stunned. Horse groceries are not cheap.

HORSES HAVE PREFERENCES AS TO THE TEXTURE OF THEIR FEED. SOME LIKE UNIFORM PELLETS. OTHERS PREFER A TRADITIONAL MIX OF WHOLE, ROLLED, OR CRACKED GRAINS, SOMETIMES WITH THE ADDITION OF MOLASSES.

One evening when Bubba and I were next door for dinner with Keith and Carole, Carole shared that she once dumped a guy because he only ate food that was white or off-white in color: pasta, white beans, wax beans, cauliflower, potatoes, onions . . . well, you get the idea. She said Keith was the next guy she dated and one reason she decided to marry him was that he ate just about everything.

"I thought if he wasn't a picky eater, he probably wouldn't be too picky about other things, either, that he'd be more laid back and steady," she said.

And that is what I've found to be true about horses. Some will only eat pelleted food, while others will only eat a traditional mix of whole, rolled, or cracked grains—sometimes with the addition of molasses. Then there are horses who are thrilled that you put anything at all in a bucket, and they slop it right up. Those horses, in my experience, are also often the ones who are more tolerant of our emotions, who will take you safely down the trail, and who don't cause much drama in the herd.

There are a few legitimate reasons why a horse might have preferences when it comes to the texture of his feed. One reason is that the texture can affect how easily the food is digested. A horse with a sensitive stomach might prefer a softer texture of feed, while a horse with a healthy stomach might be able to digest feed with a harder texture more easily.

Another reason a horse might have a preference is that texture can affect how much time they spend eating. A horse who likes to chew his food for a long time might prefer a harder texture of feed, while a horse who is more interested in eating quickly could prefer something softer.

Finally, just like our food, texture can also affect taste. A horse who has a preference for a certain taste could also have a preference for a certain texture.

If you have a horse who is a picky eater, well, I'm sorry for you. It can be a lengthy, expensive process to find a feed that meets your horse's dietary needs and is also something he'll eat. All I can suggest is to offer small amounts of different feeds to see what he likes. If you have friends who have horses, ask if you could get a handful of whatever they feed, just to try. If you have many friends who all feed something different, all the better.

Know, too, that you can soften the texture of any pelleted feed simply by adding water and waiting for the pellet to absorb it, something I like to do anyway to prevent choking. But that's just my preference. And sometimes a horse will gobble up his grain without his supplement, and his supplement without his grain, but won't eat them both together. Keep a chart of what you've tried and what doesn't work and what sort of works. That sometimes will get you to what does work. Good luck!

HORSES CAN'T VOMIT, BECAUSE A VALVE THAT LEADS TO THE STOMACH PREVENTS FOOD FROM GOING BACK INTO THE ESOPHAGUS.
This is one reason why tummy aches can be deadly to a horse who overeats, or eats bad food. Horses have an interesting digestive system. The muscles at the bottom of their esophagus are strong, and the opening to their stomach is small. That makes it hard for food to go back up the esophagus.

Plus, horses have a strong esophageal sphincter. This is the ring of muscle that closes off the opening to the stomach after food has been swallowed and helps prevent food from going back up the esophagus. Also, the stomach is high up in the horse's abdomen so it's hard for the stomach to expand enough to push food back into the esophagus. Finally, horses don't have a vomiting reflex, so they can't vomit even if they wanted to.

As you might imagine, the inability to vomit can be a problem. If a horse eats something poisonous or harmful, they can't vomit it up to get rid of it. This, under certain circumstances, can be fatal.

One time when I was in college we were at a show in Starkville, Mississippi, at the university there. I ate something that gave me food poisoning and spent most of the weekend hugging the toilet in our hotel room. As horrendous as that was, if I had not been able to vomit I'm not sure I would have survived. And yes, I realize our anatomy is quite different from that of a horse, but at least humans have two options for getting rid of bad stomach contents. Horses only have one.

If that one option, pooping, is compromised, it can have dire results. If, for example, a horse becomes constipated or his intestine twists, well let's just say it can be serious and often does not have a good ending. So if you think your horse has eaten something poisonous or gotten hold of moldy hay or unlocked the door to the feed room and helped himself to thirty-pounds of grain, by all means, call your veterinarian. Don't wait. Call now!

DESPITE BEING A VERY LARGE ANIMAL, A HORSE'S DIGESTIVE SYSTEM IS DELICATE, SO ANY CHANGE IN FEED SHOULD BE MADE ACROSS A NUMBER OF DAYS.
A sudden change to a horse's diet can upset her stomach and lead to digestive problems such as colic. For the uninitiated, colic is a giant tummy ache, and since we all know a horse can't vomit, it can be deadly.

To help prevent colic, or even a mild tummy upset, make changes to your horse's diet gradually, and increase or decrease, or mix in new feed, at a rate of no more than one pound a day. A horse who gets six pounds of grain a day would then need the change to happen over a minimum of six days. Ideally, this would take place over eight to ten days. The slower the better.

I think this slow rate of change is something people should follow, too. While our human bodies are not as sensitive as that of a horse, if I go out on a limb and decide to have dinner at an Indian restaurant, or maybe a Thai place, foods I like but normally do not eat, the next day I will invariably wish I took seven to ten days to gradually get the food into my system.

As horse owners, we're all so focused on grain that people often don't consider what a change in hay, or forage, will do to a horse's digestive tract. A study from Texas A&M University found, among other things, that changing a horse's grain diet within the previous two weeks increased the chance of colic 6.6 times. But, a change in hay within the previous two weeks was associated with an increased risk for colic of a whopping 29.5 times. Who knew?

Horses kept in stalls more than 50 percent of the time were 1.2 times more likely to colic than horses who were turned out more than 50 percent of the time. And, horses who are turned out are usually on pasture. These horses, according to the study, were significantly less likely to colic. There is something to be said for keeping a horse in an environment that <u>her</u> body is designed for. That means outside.

Our horses are outside as much as possible, but sometimes we have to place restrictions on them. Gigi, for example, usually goes into a smaller paddock, rather than a pasture. She always manages to injure herself in a bigger space, even though there is absolutely nothing out there for her to injure herself on. Cuts, scrapes, pulled muscles, bruises. Gigi manages to accumulate them all.

During show season we put our horses out at night, to keep the sun from bleaching out their coats and sunburning their noses. Sometimes during very dry or very muddy times our pastures are on rest, so as not to damage them. Or, if a horse has an injury and shouldn't be running around like Olympian Usain Bolt, then they don't get pasture time. But if you can, get your horses out in the field. Their digestive systems will thank you.

The study about forage, colic, and making feed changes very slowly, emphasizes the importance of feeding a consistent source of hay, and making gradual changes when changing feed. Also, keep in mind that mature hay has a higher fiber content. That lowers its digestibility and could be the cause of impaction colic, a really terrible situation where food gets blocked, or impacted, in the intestine. And as you may know, hay quality and maturity can fluctuate widely. We can't all buy our loads of hay from the same field for the winter season, or for the year, but if you can, do it!

TO SPOT A REAR LEG LAMENESS, LOOK TO SEE IF THE MOVEMENT OF THE HORSE IS RHYTHMIC AND EVEN ACROSS THE TOP OF THE HIPS, RATHER THAN LOOKING AT THE LEGS.
I sometimes look at horses for students and clients, and am surprised at the number of hind leg lamenesses that I see. They can be hard to spot, since most people look for the typical up and down bobbing of the head when trying to spot a lameness. That's good when looking for a front leg lameness, but a rear lameness, whether in a horse, dog, or even a barn cat, is much different.

Here, we need to watch the movement of the horse's hips. At the walk or the trot there should be an even, rhythmic movement over the top of the hips, or the portion of the back that is toward the tail. Another way to detect a rear lameness, or even a stiffness, is to see if the horse is tracking up.

Tracking up means that, at the walk, a horse will reach far enough forward with his back legs so the rear hoof lands in the hoofprint just made by the front hoof. It's even better if the horse can overtrack, meaning the rear hoof will land ahead of the print made by the front hoof.

If the horse tracks up or overtracks more on one side or the other, there could be a lameness, stiffness, soreness, or even some arthritis on the side that does not reach as far forward.

Two caveats, however. One is that a short-legged horse with a long back may be physically unable to track up or overtrack due to

For all his size, Lex has a long back and short legs, so it is harder for him to track up, yet he can whenever he is warmed up.

his poor conformation. And some gaited breeds, such as the Tennessee Walking Horse, may overtrack all the time, due to their build and general movement. In either of these two instances, watch the horse long enough to find how he usually walks, and if he is tracking evenly on both sides. A dissimilar gait left and right would concern me far more than a horse never tracking up or always overtracking.

The second caveat is to be sure to evaluate the horse after he has warmed up a bit. Any horse just pulled out of a stall, or who has been dozing in the pasture for the past several hours, may be as stiff as a board and not show his true way of walking until he has been moving for a few minutes.

A dissimilar tracking up means the horse will have a shorter stride on the lame leg, and the hip on that side might rise higher (or sometimes lower), than the other hip. The horse might also favor the affected leg by swinging it out more, away from his body, when walking or trotting.

The movement of the hind legs can also be obscured by the horse's body, so by watching the hips, you get a better idea of whether the horse is lame and which leg is affected. This is especially true when watching the swing of the leg. Sometimes a horse swinging a leg in or out farther than the other leg is just his natural way of going. I won't tell you how awkwardly I walk, and if someone ever evaluated my gait, I doubt I'd pass for sound, but I'm not in pain, and can run, jump, sit, squat, and kneel just like most of you can. It's just my weird way of going. Your horse could be just the same. Just because he walks like a duck doesn't mean he's hurting or lame.

So much to consider! But again, if you suspect your horse is lame, please call your veterinarian.

THE AVERAGE HORSE POOPS FOURTEEN TIMES A DAY AND DRINKS UP TO TWELVE GALLONS OF WATER.
Those of us who clean stalls every day might think this number is much higher. Right now, I have ten horses in the barn so that's an average of 140 poop piles every day. We also are on a well and I pity those who have horses and are paying city water bills, because I know how much water we go through.

Bubba came through the office as Lisa and I were writing this section of the book. "Poop jokes aren't my favorite kind of joke," he said, "but they're a solid number two." I have to admit, it took me a minute. Onward.

The amount of poop and water that a horse produces and drinks varies depending on a number of factors, including the horse's size, age, activity level, and diet. A horse has a very efficient digestive system, and is able to extract a lot of nutrients from her food. That's why she only needs to eat a relatively small amount of food each day, compared to her size. Sadly, we humans are not nearly as efficient as the horse. However, horses do also need to drink a lot of water to help their digestive systems function properly.

The color and consistency of a horse's poop is important because it can be a sign of their health—or lack of it. Normal horse poop is brown and firm, or it can be green and firm if they are out on pasture. If the poop is loose or watery, it can be a sign of diarrhea.

If the poop is black or tarry, it can be a sign of internal bleeding. If it comes out in tiny little balls, your horse may be constipated. Without sounding like a broken record, if you notice any changes in your horse's poop, I suggest a consult with your vet.

You already know that your horse needs access to fresh, clean water at all times. Horses can become dehydrated quickly, especially in hot weather. If you're going to be away from your horse for an extended period of time, make sure they have several ways to get water. We fill extra water troughs in the pasture, and in addition to the automatic waterers we have in the stalls, we usually also have a bucket of water if we are away for the day, just in case the automatic waterer fails. They never have, but they could, and it's not worth the risk. That's my thought anyway.

THE HORSE'S HOOF CORRESPONDS TO THE MIDDLE FINGER OF A HUMAN.
Bubba thinks it's funny that, in a way, horses are always giving us the finger. Kid humor. But in fact, horse hooves are made up of keratin, and this is the same material that makes up human fingernails and hair.

Through many, many years, all horses evolved from a common ancestor that had five toes on each foot. Over time, the toes on the outside of the foot became smaller and smaller, until they eventually disappeared. The middle toe, however, remained large and became the hoof.

This interesting evolutionary process is called "digit reduction," and is a common phenomenon in ungulates (animals who have hooves). Possibly, it developed to help horses run faster and more efficiently. In any case I've always wondered what it might be like to run across the prairie on my middle finger. I won't try it any time soon, but in the middle of the night I do wonder about it.

MANY HORSES GO BAREFOOT, BUT MANY ALSO WEAR SHOES OR REMOVABLE TRAIL BOOTS TO KEEP ROCKS FROM BRUISING THE SOLES OF THEIR HOOVES.
Most of my horses wear shoes because I can't risk one of them getting a stone bruise before an important competition. Shoes help prevent that by keeping the sole of the hoof that much farther off the ground. But do I think it's better for a horse to be barefoot? I do. We actually pull shoes when we are off-season, and when a horse is taking a break from showing, like Gigi who is taking a year to grow up and develop a brain.

Whether a horse needs shoes or not depends on a number of things, including the type of ground they will be traveling over, their workload, and their individual health. Horses who live in areas with hard, rocky terrain, or who perform strenuous activities, such as racing or jumping, could need shoes to protect their hooves from wear and tear. Horses who live on softer ground or who are not used for strenuous activities might be able to go barefoot without any problems.

Of course, once you decide to shoe the decisions don't end there, because there are several different types of shoes. The most common is a steel shoe, which is a thin piece of steel nailed to the hoof. Steel shoes are durable, but they can sometimes be heavy or make it more likely that the horse will slip on a slick surface, such as a cement barn aisle. Aluminum shoes are much lighter in weight, and can often be found on race horses.

Another type of shoe is a rubber shoe, which is made of a softer material that's less likely to cause the horse to slip. Rubber shoes are not as durable as steel, but they're lighter and can provide more shock absorption. They can also be quite a bit pricier.

Traditionally, shoes are nailed to the hoof, but sometimes they are glued on. These shoes are often made from a kind of polymer and the process can be even more expensive than rubber shoes.

Then there are a number of different types of trail boots. Trail boots are designed to protect the hoof from rocks, sticks, and other debris one might find out on the trail. They can also help keep the hoof clean and dry. <u>Sally</u> has a pair of pink ones with silver sparkles that Agnes sent her to wear on trail rides in the winter, when her shoes have been pulled. But since Sally pins her ears, glares at me, and refuses to pick up her feet when I bring them out, I get the sense that she'd rather be caught dead than wear them. If they were smaller, I'd send them back so Arabella could wear them. She looks especially good in pink sparkles.

Horse Training

Now that we understand horse behavior and know how to care for our horse, it's time to educate our equine friend. You know, each time we interact with a horse, we train him or her to act or react based on our words, body language, and emotions. That's kind of scary, if you think about it. How easy it could be to totally screw a horse up. The good news is that horses are smarter than we are, so they can usually figure out what we'd like them to do.

IT'S IMPORTANT TO RESET YOUR MIND AND EMOTIONS BEFORE INTERACTING WITH A HORSE.
Occasionally, I give my friend and neighbor, Carole Carson, riding lessons. We try to schedule them weekly when I am not at one horse competition or other, but between that, her four kids, being on the road (sometimes) with her mega-superstar husband Keith, and the modeling career she is re-starting, our lessons happen more like once a month.

The thing about Carole is that while she can often be very focused and calm, more often than not she is quite frazzled. I'll admit that she has a lot going on inside her head. But because we've had a few lessons that did not quite reach disaster status, we've started doing some mind-clearing exercises before she even walks into the barn.

Carole usually rides Bob, and as calm and forgiving as Bob is, he can tell if she is not focused, and starts to ask for leadership by committing small acts of misbehavior. He might try drifting toward the center of the arena, to me. Or, he could start jogging on his own. A horse can also pick up on a human's anxiety, and become anxious himself.

With Carole, we try to think of ocean waves, small waterfalls, and winding forest paths, because those are things that calm her and help her focus. Then we focus in on one thing: a bird walking through the sand, an interesting formation of rocks at the base of

Lex's rider and lesson team are all relaxed, which gives him the confidence he needs to relax and become engaged in his lesson.

the waterfall, or a beautiful leaf on a tree. Only when she can focus and admire that one single thing, will I let her walk inside the barn, because I know then, that she is not thinking about her son's poor report card, or what she should wear to the upcoming country music awards, or if her oldest has enough friends. I know she is emotionally able to focus on her horse and on her lesson, and that she will have a great ride.

HORSES DISTINGUISH TONES AND VOWEL SOUNDS RATHER THAN WORDS.
This is so important to know. What it means is that saying no, go, slow, toe, so, oh, hello, or low in a firm tone will probably produce a swift halt in your equine friend's forward motion.

When I was in college at Middle Tennessee State University, one of my classmates was loping a retired reining horse in the indoor arena. For those not familiar with reining, it's a Western, cowboy kind of sport that incorporates sliding stops, spins, lead changes, circles and more to demonstrate a horse's handiness. Anyway, someone walked into the arena and my classmate called out, "Hello!" The next thing I knew, the horse planted his butt into the ground and performed an epic sliding stop. The rider, of course, somersaulted over the horse's head and landed in the dirt. For his part, the horse did exactly what he thought he was supposed to do. He heard a long O sound and knew that meant to stop.

Darcy tells me that in her therapeutic riding program the horses are trained to certain voice commands. Because the vowels in walk and trot can sound similar to a horse, the center uses "walk on." That way the horse hears an a/o vowel combination, which is different to them than one sound or the other.

Lisa tells of a British woman who came to volunteer with her horses and was having trouble getting the horses to canter in the round pen because she asked the horses to "can-TAH" instead of "canter." Once they had worked together to Americanize the woman's accent, at least for a few words, the horses better understood her and readily complied.

In addition to accent, the tone and pitch of the voice is important. Jon has an average-pitched voice for a man, meaning his voice is deeper than that of most women, but he is generally soft spoken. There is something in the delivery of his words, however, that's firm and distinct, even though he rarely speaks loudly, even to the horses. A man with a loud, very deep voice can be heard very differently than a teen-aged girl, even though they might have the same accent and be speaking their vowel sounds in much the same manner.

Why is this all this important? Well, we all want to communicate with our horses. At least I hope we all do. And understanding that the horse hears and reacts to the vowel sound can be an important tool in that communication. Most horses want to please us, and when they don't, it often is due to a communication error—and that is on us. The same word said in the same tone of voice with the same facial expression and body language goes a long way toward communicating a clear intention to your horse.

Remember that many horses in their teen years and older have some form of hearing loss. They might not hear certain sounds or frequencies, so if you say "whoa" in a normal tone of voice and a normal volume, for example, your horse may hear just fine and understand very well what he is supposed to do. But "whoa" shouted in a higher pitch along with frantic body language may confuse your horse. He may not hear the higher tone and interpret your body language to mean the zombie apocalypse has finally arrived and his only thought is to run as fast as possible away from the danger you so clearly just communicated to him.

There is a wealth of information to discover here, but for the sake of time and brevity, do a bit of research of your own. Spend some time with your horse to discover what he does and does not seem to hear, and then adjust your verbal instructions to him accordingly. And, before you punish your horse, consider the fact that he just may not hear you clearly, or understand what you want him to do.

TO RAISE OR LOWER YOUR HORSE'S ENERGY, BREATHE IN RHYTHM WITH HIM, THEN GRADUALLY BREATHE SLIGHTLY FASTER OR SLOWER, DEPENDING ON WHETHER YOU WANT AN INCREASE OR DECREASE.
A few months ago, I was watching Darcy lead a rider in a therapeutic riding lesson. The rider was anxious, and her anxiety was beginning to transfer to her horse. Darcy's eyes started to dart around, like they always do when she's not quite sure what to do, and the sidewalker, the person who walks along side the rider to help interpret the instructor's words (and also sometimes to lend physical support) was also tense. I could tell because she started taking these teensy steps and the expression on her face made me think she might

just have swallowed a bug. But no. She was also quite unsure what to do.

Fortunately, the instructor had a plan for this very thing, and brought everyone to a halt. She approached the rider, and even though I strained my ears trying to listen in, I couldn't hear exactly what she said to the rider, Darcy, and the sidewalker. But all of a sudden all of them were taking in big, deep breaths, and slowly letting them out. The third time they did this, the horse, ever a herd animal and wanting so badly to be part of the fun, also let out a big sigh. Then everyone laughed, and a potentially bad moment was averted.

It was a good reminder that you can raise or lower your horse's energy, just by raising or lowering your own. Your horse wants to be a herd with you, and should so respect your leadership, that she will match her thoughts, feelings, and emotions to yours. That is what being a prey animal is. And, that level of connectivity is the result of great leadership.

REMEMBER TO REWARD YOUR HORSE'S THOUGHTS AND INTENTIONS.
We all like to be praised for our efforts, even if we do not fully get it right. Horses are no different. A little scratch on the neck for walking over the scary tarp, even if the walk didn't look all that pretty, goes a long way toward developing eventual perfection. There is nothing worse than trying—and not being recognized for the effort.

That happens with me whenever I try to cook dinner. It never turns out the way I envision, but I do plan the meal and put a lot of love into it. It makes me want to try harder whenever Bubba or

Darcy thank me, or find something nice to say about my effort, even though I know they secretly are shoving forkfuls of food onto the floor for Hank, our part-Beagle (and stick-carrying guard dog) to eat. And they think I don't know.

It's easy for us humans to focus on the negative, to think about what our horse didn't do, or what we and our horse did not accomplish together. But if you turn that thought cattywampus and focus on the tiny baby steps you did accomplish, it will make all the difference. Jon is especially good at this, and I have learned much from him in this area. He has taught me to reward every positive, so I know that if you reward every try, your horse will make an even bigger effort for you next time.

DESENSITIZING IS NEVER ABOUT SCARING HORSES. INSTEAD, IT IS ABOUT MAKING HORSES COMFORTABLE IN ALL THE UNUSUAL SITUATIONS THE HUMAN WORLD PUTS THEM IN.

Horses were never designed to experience all that they do today. They were designed to graze, roam the prairie, drink from creeks and streams, and rarely, if ever, see a human being. Today, most horses experience the sights, sounds, and movements of motor vehicles; lots of people; music from a radio or other player; and so much more. They see tarps that cover piles of hay, umbrellas, and people riding, of all things, a bicycle. For a prey animal, any one of these experiences can be unsettling. Several of them together can be downright frightening.

That's where desensitizing comes in. Unfortunately, some trainers have given the concept a bad name, because they use the idea to frighten a horse into compliance, rather than gently accustom a horse to many different sights, sounds, and movements that the horse can then categorize as safe.

Desensitizing should start with gently and repeatedly tossing something like a saddle pad alongside a horse's flank, until he realizes that this will in no way hurt him. It can then progress to all of the sounds and objects a horse might see in the course of his duties. A ranch horse might see and hear semi-trucks and big-truck horns. An event horse will see lots of shapes and colors on jumps, while a 4-H project horse might experience lots of people and horses moving around on the outside of the show area, along with the loud speaker and maybe a slew of younger siblings running and playing nearby.

Tessie is allowed to explore this tarp at her own pace and could walk away, but she chooses to stay and investigate.

Some horses are naturally more secure and accepting of their surroundings and do not need much in the way of desensitization. We've mentioned Bob. For him, becoming frightened and spooking is way too much effort, and he spends precious energy he could be using to sleep. On the other hand, Gigi thinks every single thing in the entire universe was put there specifically for her to spook at. Such fun!

There might also, on occasion, be a few things your horse never becomes desensitized or accustomed to. A horse I rode as a teen was terrified of white plastic grocery bags. Yellow, blue, and gray ones were of no concern, but whenever I was around the horse, I always had to keep an eye out for those terrifying white bags, because if he saw one, he'd run the opposite direction faster than a rat scurrying up a drainpipe.

Looking back, it might have been that the horse could not see the bags clearly. I didn't understand back then that, to a horse, whites can look as bright as a solar eclipse. Because he could not see what the bag was, he became frightened and ran. While this was annoying (and a little scary at times), better to know what the horse's trigger was, than not.

The sheer terror of plastic grocery bags aside, there are two main take-aways here. One, only go as fast or slow as your horse tells you he is ready for. Desensitizing is all about his time frame, not yours. And two, never intentionally or unintentionally frighten your horse. Watch the body language and stop, or at least reduce the pressure, as soon as your horse tells you he is emotionally uncomfortable or unsure.

A HORSE CANNOT PHYSICALLY PICK UP HIS HOOF FOR IT TO BE CLEANED IF HE IS STANDING WITH MOST OF HIS WEIGHT ON THAT LEG.

If you have ever tried to pick up a horse's hoof and it felt like you were trying to lift the Statue of Liberty, you probably were trying to lift the horse's hoof while she was bearing weight on that leg.

Imagine yourself standing, unless of course you already are. Now think of yourself as balancing most of your weight on your left leg. Most of us do this when we are waiting in line, or standing for a period of time. We put more weight on one leg or the other and then shift our weight back and forth. Horses do this, too.

Back to the left leg. Now imagine someone coming up and trying to lift your left foot off the ground. Unless they are a weight lifter, it will nearly be impossible. It will be much easier for someone to lift your right leg, because all your weight is on the left.

When it comes to picking up your horse's hoof, the good news is there is an easy solution. As you stand next to the horse's left front shoulder with your face looking toward the horse's tail, run your

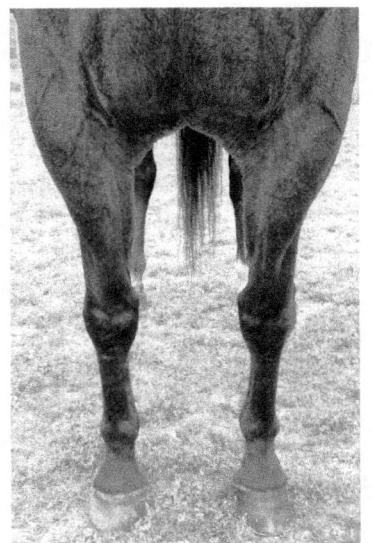

Quincy is standing with even weight on both front legs.

hand down the horse's left front leg, lean your shoulder into the horse's shoulder and upper leg, and most likely she will shift her weight to the other leg.

Or, you can do as Lisa does and always pick out your horse's feet in the same order. She does left front, left rear, and then right front and right rear, and most of the time her horses lift the next foot in the order before she even gets there. Makes the job easy, but Lisa says you have to be 100 percent consistent about the order to give your horse the unfailing dependability needed to anticipate your next move.

WHEN BACKING, BE AWARE OF WHICH FRONT LEG THE HORSE HAS THE MOST WEIGHT ON, THEN ASK THE HORSE TO MOVE THE OTHER LEG BACK. THIS WORKS BOTH FROM THE GROUND AND UNDER SADDLE.

This is along the same lines as the previous thought, but is somewhat more involved. The same concept of weight and picking up feet is involved when you ask your horse to back. Whenever I go to look at a horse for one of my riding students, or for an owner, one thing I always ask the horse to do is back up. I do this for a few reasons. One is that if the horse physically can't back, or can only do so with difficulty or reluctance, it could mean there is soreness or even arthritis that will prohibit the horse from performing at the level the owner or rider expects.

Another reason is if the horse looks as if he can physically go in reverse, but won't, then the horse either has very poor manners, or is uneducated. Both can be red flags under certain circumstances.

The final reason a horse might refuse to back, is that the human is asking the horse to first move the leg that is currently bearing the most weight. Keep in mind that a true backward gait is a reverse trot. Right front and left rear will move backward as a diagonal pair of legs, and the left front and right rear will then move backward as the second diagonal pair.

So how do you tell on what leg a horse is weight bearing? If you take the time to spend just a few minutes watching your horse (or other horses) stand, you should figure it out. Look at the joints. Which knee seems compressed, and which seems looser? Is the horse leaning in one direction more than the other? Think of yourself. If you are weight bearing on your left leg, your upper body will slant slightly that direction.

The rear legs are somewhat easier to discern, since often a horse will rest a back foot. If that happens, because the back is a diagonal gait, assume the horse is also bearing less weight on the diagonal front leg. When a horse is resting the left hind, less weight is on the diagonal right front, so the horse is probably weight bearing on the left front. Get down on all fours and try it. Seriously. Do it!

Two caveats here. Bubba wanted me to remind you that it is possible that a horse is evenly balanced and carrying an even amount of weight on both front legs (or both hind legs). The other situation is that each horse is an individual, and due to build, weight, injury, personal preference, and a host of other reasons, a horse may not conform to any of the above-mentioned rules of thumb. That's why it's important to spend time watching your horse stand. Once you know how your horse stands, you'll have a better understanding of which leg to ask to move first when asking for the back, and what to do to get your horse to pick up his feet.

A TRAIL HORSE HAS TO BE SURE-FOOTED, SENSIBLE, PATIENT, GET ALONG WITH OTHER HORSES, AND HAVE AN EASY-GOING TEMPERAMENT TO BE SUITED FOR THE JOB.
One of my (many) pet peeves is people who take horses out on the trail who just are not suited for the job. If your horse is as crazy as a soup sandwich, don't take her trail riding. Instead, take a few months, or a year, and do the appropriate groundwork to build your horse's confidence in herself and in you. Round penning, ground driving, leading exercises, and being consistent with rules about manners will all go a long way toward eventually getting your horse to safely and quietly mosey down the trail.

Know, though, that some horses are just not going to be the safe, quiet trail horse you desire, no matter what you do. As Agnes says, "You can't turn a pump handle into a pig." Whether it's their inherent temperament, past handling, or past experiences, some horses need to stay home.

Years ago, when I was a teen working at a boarding stable, there was an older girl who had a palomino and white Paint. It was a beautiful horse and even though I can't remember if it was a mare or a gelding or what the horse's name was, I'll always remember that this horse was so unpredictable it made him (for convenience, let's decide he was a gelding) dangerous. This horse would behave beautifully every day for two to three weeks, and then, boom!, he'd spook so hard at a wheelbarrow that he might fall over. Or, a car's horn would honk in the driveway, and this horse would bolt so badly he'd crash through fences. Then he'd be fine for another few weeks.

Obviously, there was something going on in this horse's brain. And just like some people, I have seen some horses who are mentally or emotionally unstable.

On the other hand, Lisa had a horse when she was a teen who was terrified of the sound of a car honk. He could help earn her a high-point all-around rider championship at a show one day and the next day a car would honk way out in the parking lot and he'd run as if a herd of elephants suddenly trampled through the pasture. Fortunately, Lisa also worked at the time at a dude ranch and all those horses did was go down a trail, nose to tail with the horse in front and behind, so she sold him to one of the trail guides there.

Spike enjoys his trail time and is a safe, steady, and dependable equine partner.

Back then, there were never honking cars on the remote trails along the Minnesota River, and the horse had a good career there.

It all goes back to what Agnes said: A pig cannot be a pump handle, and vice versa. Your top barrel racer might not be best suited as a jumper. Your kids' pony, who does so wonderfully in the riding ring, might not be the safest mount two miles down the trail. Nurture what you have. By all means bring your horse to his best potential, but always keep in mind what his natural physical, mental, cognitive, and emotional strengths and weaknesses are. If you can do that, you and your horse will both be much happier.

IF A NORMALLY SENSIBLE HORSE REFUSES A JUMP OR TRAIL OBSTACLE, IT MIGHT BE UNSAFE, OR IT MIGHT BE THAT SHE CANNOT SEE IT PROPERLY.

Most horses are so very willing to please. If they do not do as we ask, there most often is a good reason. Possibly, the horse had a bad experience previously with something similar. I don't like heights because when I was small, a footbridge I was walking over almost collapsed. It was a terrifying experience for my six-year-old self. If your horse will not go through water, well, then he may have slipped previously. Or, maybe he can sense an uneven depth, or there is moss on the rocky bottom and he knows it will be unsafe to cross.

If the water is in direct sunlight, your horse might not be able to see much of it at all, especially if you've just come out of the woods. Remember that it can take up to fifteen minutes for a horse's eye to adjust to changing light and dark, while our eyes adjust far more quickly. Sometimes just standing before an obstacle for a few minutes will allow your horse to mentally process the challenge, and also see it more clearly.

But always, trust your horse. If your horse tells you she would rather swim through a lake filled with piranhas, understand that today is not the day to push the issue. Then, check the obstacle for safety. Imagine the scenario from your horse's perspective. What does your horse see, hear, or smell that makes her feel unsafe? Use your brain to problem solve, and then, when you and your horse are both ready, try again using baby steps and lots of positive praise.

LEAD ROPES DON'T LEAD HORSES.
I have been saying this as long as I can remember. I don't know where I first heard it, and for the longest time I didn't really understand what it meant. One instructor from many years back said I should think about it, and that eventually the meaning would come to me. It took a while, more than a decade actually, but to my surprise, he was absolutely right.

A few years ago I was doing an interview with my friends Glenn Hebert and Jamie Jennings on the podcast *Horses in the Morning*, and we were talking about a poison that a murderer had sent to my barn. It was in the form of something a horse would eat, and I wanted to let horse owners know to be sure they knew what was in their horse's pasture, hay, grain, and supplements, because most people don't take time to educate themselves about these kinds of things.

Anyway, right smack in the middle of the interview it came to me, what lead ropes don't lead horses actually means. Why all those years of pondering should come to fruition when I was live on the air, I don't know, but it did, and what I discovered was this: Your horse chooses to walk with you, and no amount of pulling or yanking on a lead rope can entice her to do so. She has to want to come with you. She has to believe you are her leader and that you will keep her safe, no matter what horrible creature might jump out and try to eat her, no matter that there is an earthquake and the world is splitting apart. She has to respect and trust you in all instances, and in all circumstances. And none of that will happen unless you understand horse behavior and communication, and consistently act in a manner that is deserving of her respect.

Everything we have discussed so far in this book brings us right to this thought: Lead ropes don't lead horses. You do.

Finally, we get to the fun part! I know most people love to ride, although Lisa tells me some of you find just as much enjoyment doing groundwork with your horses. I hope you folks will read on, because even though this section focuses on mounted activities, there are a few important things here for you, too.

THE BEST TEACHERS OF HORSEMANSHIP ARE HORSES.
This is so true. I love to watch herd behavior and can sit for hours watching our horses in their pasture. When Sally pins her ears, sticks out her chin, and makes an ugly face at Bob when he grazes too close, it's a sign she doesn't want company. And when Bob moves away, it also tells me that Sally is Bob's herd leader. He yielded his personal space to her, so she is the dominant one in charge. That and a thousand other ways our horses communicate can teach us much, if we are open to it.

Every time we interact with a horse, we teach the horse something. But more important, the horse teaches something to us—if we are smart enough to learn. Horsemanship surrounds the riding, training, and care of horses, and if done correctly, helps us build a closer relationship with our equine friends.

You can read a book like this, watch a video, or go to a clinic and watch an expert work with a horse, but there is no better teacher of horsemanship than the horse. I liken this process of learning to an infant learning language. If you watch closely, a baby, or even a toddler, watches older children and adults. From this watching they learn language, behavior; and to interpret facial expressions, body movement, and tone of voice.

We watch our horses, but what do we learn about them and about ourselves from that watching? Lisa's youth mare, a little Appaloosa named Snoqualmie, was often hard to catch. But, over time, Lisa learned that if Snoqualmie turned to face her, even if she was three hundred feet away, and then dropped her head a fraction of an inch, it meant she was ready to be caught. Lisa could walk right up to her. If Lisa kept on "chasing" her, however, as kids often do, Snoqualmie would easily gallop away. From that experience, Lisa learned to be observant, and to react to the signal her horse was giving her, rather than be the instigator of another insane hour of running around the pasture.

Like people, some horses are better communicators and teachers than others. A horse I recently had in training, Ringo, liked to buck, just once or twice in the first five minutes of our riding session. He also did this when he was turned out into the paddock. For him it meant, "I'm so happy! This is great! Let's have some fun together!" He never bucked hard; it was more of a kick up his heels kind of a thing, and then he settled down to business.

Over time I learned that if Ringo didn't buck, he was having an off day. Our training sessions were never as good, and he never felt quite right under saddle. Fortunately, those days were rare. Would Ringo be a horse for everyone? Of course not, but he went on to become <u>one</u> of the Appaloosa breed's rare four-time medallion winners, winning national championships in halter, racing, performance, and distance riding. Now he is having fun herding cattle somewhere across the West Texas plains.

Horsemanship is learning to care for your horse physically, psychologically, and emotionally. It's learning to ride in balance and harmony with your horse, and to give consistent cues that your horse understands. Horsemanship is understanding that a horse is a horse, and not a dog, or a human. It's knowing that a horse wants to be treated as a horse and that the horse is inherently different from every other species on the planet. Horsemanship is all of that and only comes with the understanding that every day, every single time you see, watch, or interact with a horse, you and he will both learn something about each other. Only the horse can teach you that, but you have to be ready to learn.

THE AVERAGE HEALTHY HORSE CAN CARRY 20 PERCENT OF HIS OR HER BODY WEIGHT, INCLUDING TACK, SO A 1,000 LB. HORSE COULD CARRY UP TO 200 LBS.
As a side note, a 1,000 lb. racehorse carries 11-12.6 percent of body weight when racing, or 110-126 lbs. So yes, there's a lot of leeway here, but these figures are good places to start. I gave a clinic a few years ago and one rider in my balanced riding session must have

weighed 250 pounds. His poor little horse was a narrow 14.2 hand three-year-old Spotted Saddlehorse who was displaying many behavioral problems. When asked to go, he raised his <u>head</u> and pinned his ears. After going, he kicked out several times. Obviously, the problem was that the man (who was also riding in a huge western saddle that probably weighed forty pounds) was too heavy for his horse. Most likely making matters worse, the heavy saddle did not fit the horse. This is such a tough area for me, to tell a rider that he or she is causing their horse to become sore because they are too heavy for their horse. But sometimes I have to pull up my big girl panties and say the words.

Unfortunately, our horses can't simply say, "Hey, this saddle doesn't fit and you're too heavy." Our horses use body language instead of words. Some exhibit the behaviors listed above. Others will buck or snap their teeth. And yet others, stoic saints they are, will do the best they can, but you might notice they are walking slower, or that they struggle to pick up their feet to get themselves, and you, over a small log across the trail.

One key issue here is that we often don't know how much a horse weighs. There are a few solutions to that, however. One is that your local county agricultural extension agent may have a set of livestock scales he or she can bring out. Then there is the issue of getting your horse to stand on the scale, but that is probably a topic for another book. Suffice to say, mostly, if a horse will load into a trailer, they will usually stand on a livestock scale.

Another option is your local feed mill (not a suburban farm store, although I have nothing against them, but usually they do not have a set of scales). But a feed mill will and if you ask nicely and bring doughnuts maybe they will let you trailer your horse in to stand on their scales.

A third option is to purchase your own set of scales. If you own a boarding facility or have a lot of horses, this might be a wise investment, but if you only have a few horses, the several thousands of dollars such a scale costs might not be worth it.

If none of these options work for you, then you will just have to guestimate. Sally Blue will kill me if she ever finds out I told you, but she weighs 1250 pounds. She is a 15.2 hand stocky Appaloosa mare. Darcy's Petey, is taller and slimmer, but weighs in at 1300 pounds. We've just talked about Lisa's youth mare, Snoqualmie. She weighed 850 pounds (as per the scales at the local feed mill in Maple Plain, Minnesota).

Do the math. If you think your healthy middle-aged horse weighs a thousand pounds, then you and your saddle should together weigh two hundred pounds or less. Very young horses, older horses, or horses who carry unbalanced riders, should step down from 20 percent of their body weight to about 16 percent.

But here's the thing, if you are tuned in to your horse's body language, she will tell you if she is struggling. She will act out, or her performance under saddle will be less. Remember too, that the weight your horse carries is you, and your saddle and pad combined, so switching from a heavy western saddle to a light-weight endurance saddle or a lighter English saddle can make all the difference—as long as the saddle fits your horse and is comfortable for you, of course.

But, knowing how much, exactly, your horse weighs will also help you calculate the optimum amount of feed and supplements to give, which means you are being thrifty and also not over- or under-feeding your horse.

LIKE FINDING A GOOD PAIR OF SHOES THAT FIT YOU WELL, FINDING A SADDLE THAT FITS BOTH HORSE AND RIDER CAN BE VERY DIFFICULT.
Years ago, a saddle was all about the rider. Was the seat big enough, but not too big? Did the stirrups hang in the right place so the rider was balanced? Did the rise of the front and the back of the saddle

This cute saddle didn't fit any of the horses at Colby's Army.

give the rider enough support, but not be so confining it was hard to mount and dismount? And my "favorite" criteria: did the saddle look fabulous with the horse and rider? Ugh. Really? Those are all points to consider (except the last one, unless you are showing in higher-level competition), but not one of them considers the horse.

Fortunately, in recent years saddle selection has finally become mostly about the horse. I am not a certified saddle fitter, but I've taken time to educate myself about fitting saddles, because delivering a good-fitting saddle to your horse is one of the nicest things you can do. Sally even "told" Agnes that a good saddle fit makes her happier than getting a handful of peppermints.

In getting a good fit, it's best to start at the beginning, and that's with the saddle's condition. Be sure the stitching is tight, that each piece of leather or synthetic material the saddle is made of is in good condition, and that there are no lumps on the underside that might cause your horse pain, such as a screw head loosening up from the saddle tree, the interior frame the saddle is built around.

Then put the pommel (the front of the saddle) down on a pad or protective piece of carpeting with the back of the saddle sticking upright. Now look down the seat of the saddle. Is there a straight line from the center of the cantle (the back of the saddle) along the seat to the center of the pommel? Or, is there a twist? If there is a twist it could mean an uneven or a broken tree, which will be both uncomfortable and unsafe for you and your horse. And, it will cause you to ride crookedly, which is about as fun as oral surgery.

Lastly, place the cantle on your hip and pull gently, but steadily, on the pommel. If wrinkles appear in the seat, this could be another sign that the tree is damaged. If this is the case, have an expert take a look at it.

If you have a western saddle, be sure to check the horn. If it's loose, that's yet another indication that the saddle is not in good enough shape to ride in. It's sometimes possible to fix a loose horn, but this kind of saddle also makes a great wall ornament. Or, I've seen amazing photos on Pinterest of saddles painted to look like rose gardens or waterfalls.

Be sure, too, to inspect the flocking (the fleece on the underside of a western saddle) for even wear and quality of condition.

Also, on the underside of any saddle, check the width of the gullet. That's the deep groove that goes down the center of the saddle from front to back. On many of the more inexpensive saddles, the gullet is either too narrow for the horse's spine, or it narrows toward the back. Why would a saddle maker do that? I have no idea. However, suffice to say if the gullet is too narrow, it will be uncomfortable for your horse, and can cause soreness.

By this time, you know that soreness can cause behavior problems. Don't worry, though. Just paint those narrow-gulleted saddles and hang them on your wall right next to the saddles with loose horns and broken trees. Or, you could even make some cool bar stools out of them.

Assuming the condition of the saddle checks out well, the next step is to place the saddle on your horse's back without any pads. Pads can mask the true fit of a saddle, so it's easier to check the fit without them. Also, don't worry about doing up the cinch or girth. Instead, just let the saddle sit on your horse's back.

I like my horses to stand square when I fit a saddle to them. If they're resting a back leg, or posing like a ballerina, it can bunch and stretch muscles and mask the true fit. To check the fit:

1. Put your fist into the opening between your horse's withers and the front of the saddle. If you can't fit it in (assuming you have a normal-sized hand), the saddle sits too low on his back. The exception here is an English cutback saddle, which has an opening for the withers.

2. If you look at the saddle from the side, the seat should be level. English or western, it doesn't matter. If the seat tilts forward or back, the saddle will pitch the rider in the same direction. Some leveling can be done with a "bump" pad that raises up the back of the saddle, but that often tightens the fit in the horse's shoulder. And then the back of the saddle can start to bounce up and down like a demented yoyo. So forget the bump pad. When you put the saddle on your horse's back, the seat should be level.

3. Then, make your hand flat, and stick your fingers as far as you can under the front of the saddle. Start at the top where the saddle first makes contact with your horse, just under the wither area, and run your hand all the way down. If at any point your feel a lot of pressure, or pinching, the saddle is too tight for your friend. This is the number one area where I feel saddles do not fit. They most often are too tight in the shoulder. But maybe that's because I have horses that are a little too well-fed.

4. Be sure also to look under the saddle where your knee would lie, and also behind your thigh. Does the saddle fit nice and flat along

your horse's side? Or does it stick out and form a gap? If there is a gap, or bridging, the saddle is probably too wide, or it could have been damaged by being stored improperly. As Jon always says, "A good saddle rack can be worth more than the saddle." If the saddle bridges, it will not provide enough support to stay in place and may tip or rock—and that can be unsafe to you as a rider, while also making your horse miserable.

5. Under where your hips would be on the sides of the saddle, it should also fit snugly with no gaps or "bridging," and also no undue tightness.

6. The back of the saddle should neither dig into the horse's spine (which many western saddles do), or tip up so there is no contact (typical of English saddles). With an English saddle, you should also be able to see daylight all the way through the gullet, or underside of the saddle, along the horse's spine.

7. With everything we have discussed here, be sure to check the fit on both the left and right sides. Over time, and depending on their job, a horse can build up more muscle on one side of his body than on the other. This means a specific saddle might fit on the left side, but not on the right, or vice versa. To fit correctly, a saddle must fit the horse well on both sides.

Every saddle manufacturer and every saddle fitter will have their own tweaks to basic saddle fit, but the concepts, whether you ride western or English, are the same. And here's the thing: 90 percent of you are going to go out to the barn and check the saddle fit and find your saddle doesn't even come close to fitting your horse. Don't feel too bad about it. I've been there more times than I care to discuss. The good news is you now know what you have to do, and yes, it will cost some money, but your horse will be so grateful to finally be wearing a saddle that is comfortable that your relationship with him and his performance for you will both improve. (Until he gains or loses weight or muscle tone, and all of a sudden, the saddle no longer fits. But that's a problem for another day.)

CHECK THE TIGHTNESS OF A GIRTH OR CINCH BETWEEN THE HORSE'S LEGS, NOT ON THE HORSE'S SIDE, AS THE THICKNESS OF THE SADDLE PAD CAN GIVE A FALSE READING.
A horse is considered "girthy" when he pins his ears, snaps his teeth, stomps his feet, and/or swishes his tail when being saddled, and when the girth or cinch is tightened. And FYI, if you're not an experienced horse person and are only reading this because you like the Cat Enright mysteries, or like me, think Keith Carson is a hunk and are hoping for a glimpse of him here, girth is the English style of riding's term for the strap that goes under the horse's belly and keeps the saddle on. Cinch is the term for the same strap on a western saddle.

My horses are not girthy. Period. They just aren't. And it's because of two reasons. One, we take great care when girthing or cinching our horses. We go slowly, and only very gently tighten the strap one hole at a time. And we never jerk or yank the strap. I see that happen so often, and when I do, I want to go over to the person and ask if they would like someone tightening their belt like that?

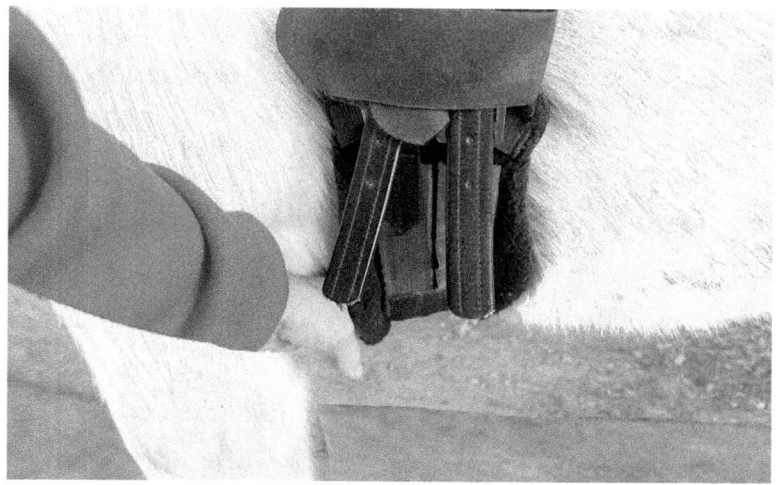

Spike's girth is comfortably snug.

Would that be comfortable? Pleasant? Would they be best friends with the person who did that to them?

The second reason our horses are not girthy is because we check the tightness of the girth/cinch between the horse's front legs, versus on the horse's side. Because the thickness of the saddle pad can pull the top of the girth or cinch away from the horse's side, if you check the tightness there, you might think the girth was too loose. Riding in a saddle with a loose girth or cinch is not a good thing, because if the saddle slips sideways, so do you. I've tried that a time or two, and really can't recommend it. But if you tighten the girth because it feels loose on the side, it could become so tight the horse may have trouble expanding his chest to breathe. Probably, if I was a horse, that would feel like I was wearing a corset.

Instead, slip your fingers between the horse's front legs to check tightness. While the girth might seem loose on the side, it could feel quite snug between the horse's legs. You will get a truer reading doing it this way, and your horse will be much happier.

THE SAFEST WAY TO RIDE A HORSE THROUGH A GATE IS TO PUSH THE GATE THE SAME DIRECTION YOU'RE GOING.
We've all been there. Well, those of us who trail ride or compete in trail classes have. One: you need to get through a gate on the trail and don't want to dismount. Or, two, the trail class requires you to navigate the gate from atop your horse, but you can't figure out the best way to get through. Granted, some gates have tricky approaches and others have weird latches that require creative maneuvering, but most gates will open best if you push the gate the direction you are going. This is true if you are mounted, leading your horse through a gate, or just walking through it yourself.

I have seen more trail classes lost because the rider cannot figure out how to get through the gate. With most competitive classes, I like to be the first rider in the ring—or the second, depending on how confident my horse is. But not trail. I like to watch other riders go first so I can learn from their mistakes.

Usually the rider rushes the approach and then does not allow the horse time to settle next to the gate, so the horse is unsure what is to come next. Then if the rider pulls the gate toward them, there is that awkward moment of trying to get the horse's hind end through and still hold on to the gate.

If you are on the ground it's also quite awkward to pull the gate toward you, keep your hand on the gate (so in theory the other horses and cows don't get out), then turn the horse around so you can close the gate. Pushing a gate away from you makes it easier to hold on to, and also get your horse through smoothly and safely.

IN EVERY STYLE OF RIDING, A TWO-POINT (WHERE THE RIDER'S SEAT IS ELEVATED FROM THE SADDLE AND THE UPPER BODY IS BALANCED OVER THE RIDER'S LEGS WITH THE HEELS DOWN) DEVELOPS BALANCE, CORE STRENGTH, AND PROPER LEG POSITION.

The two-point is "it" when it comes to riding, but there are a few things you should learn first. No matter what style you ride, if you're looking at a photo of yourself, your shoulder, hip and heel should be in a vertical line, and your knee and toe should also be in a vertical line. I'm also going to throw in that your hand, arm, and elbow should be in a straight line from where the reins attach to the horse's bit, bosal, or sidepull. It's all about the angles.

Depending on the build of your horse, your saddle, and how proportionate your arms and legs are to your body, you can vary these angles a teensy bit either way, but this is exactly what you need to stay balanced and on top of your horse.

Now let's add in keeping your heels down. First, this is a huge safety measure, because when your heels are down, it should prevent your foot from sliding through the stirrup. At the program where Darcy volunteers, they use safety stirrups, where the outside of the stirrup is essentially a large, thick, rubber band. (She says sometimes they use pony-tail bands.) In any case, the band will come loose if too much pressure is put on it, and the rider's foot will fall free of the stirrup in an emergency. Pretty cool idea!

But the reality is that most of us do not ride with safety stirrups (even though some of us really should). There are both English and western versions by the way, just in case you think you might be one of those people who should be riding in them, but are using the excuse that you ride western and they don't make them for western saddles. Those stirrups look a little different from English safety stirrups, but they do work.

Let's go back to the angles. If, when seated, your shoulder, hip, and heel are aligned, and your knee and toe are in the right place with your toes higher than your heel, you can do something called a two-point, which is essentially lifting your butt out of the saddle and balancing as you ride.

Why might you want to do that, you ask? Look at photos or videos of people who are jumping, riding endurance, or roping calves. They all regularly perform a two-point. But even if you don't want to climb a vertical hill with your horse in the middle of a fifty-

This rider practices a two-point with her legs underneath her.

mile ride, being able to perform a two-point whether at the standstill, the walk, the trot, or the canter, means that you are riding in balance with your horse.

That, my friends, is the key. If you are in balance with your horse, you should not fall off. (Unless you are a trick rider or have a death wish, I think the goal for most of us is to actually stay on the horse.) You also will make it easier for your horse to carry you, and hopefully can prevent sore spots on your horse's back from developing.

If you cannot get up out of the saddle and hold a two-point, most likely your lower legs are too far forward. Sit down, bring your lower legs back underneath your body (but not too far or you will tip yourself forward), make sure your heels are down, squeeze lightly with your thighs, and then raise yourself up into the two-point. Please be sure you do not balance yourself with your reins. It's perfectly acceptable (in my opinion) to put your hands on top of the horse's neck, partway between the saddle and the horse's ears. Please do that for balance instead of pulling on your horse's face.

You don't have to come all the way up out of the saddle either. In fact, you shouldn't. Instead, keep some bend in your knee, and when you can balance well enough to start moving, let all your weight sink to your heels, and use them as a shock absorber. When you sit down, your horse will thank you if you do so slowly. Put yourself into your horse's shoes and imagine how you would feel if someone repeatedly thumped down on your back. Remember that, if needed, you can grab a handful of mane to slow yourself down when going back to a sitting position.

Make sure, too, that your toes are not turned out too far. Several things happen when you do that. One, when your toes turn out, your heels go into the horse and you may end up going somewhat faster than you had hoped. Then, when your toes turn out, so does your knee and thigh, and you lose contact with your saddle because, sadly, all your gripping muscles are gripping air, instead of the saddle.

My co-author says I am getting to the point in a round-about way, but trust me, I'm getting there. We've talked about the benefits of a two-point when it comes to balance and leg position, but it also helps your core strength. Core strength comes from the trunk of your body, the middle section. If you do not have enough core strength, you can't sit the trot, and instead will bounce all over your horse's back and make her both uncomfortable and mad—and you'll feel like you rode in the back of a dump truck instead of on your horse. Core strength is critical to all we do, from leaning down to tie your shoes (and getting back up) to being sure you can engage your tummy muscles and stick tight to the saddle at a trot or lope.

So, two-point, people. Two-point. You will hate it at first, but I promise it will become your new best friend. (And it's way easier than posting without stirrups.)

THE SEQUENCE OF FOOTFALLS FOR THE HORSE AT THE WALK IS LEFT HIND, LEFT FRONT, RIGHT HIND, RIGHT FRONT.
It absolutely amazes me the number of really good riders who do not understand how their horse moves. At the walk it is left hind, left front, right hind, right front. Think it, watch it, get down on

your hands and knees and do it yourself. Seriously. This is the way every horse walks. If you go through the motions of doing it yourself, you will better and more quickly understand it. Truly, you will. I do suggest that you try this in a more private place, though, and not, for example, at your favorite coffee bar or local shopping mall.

This left, left, right, right way of walking is called a lateral gait, since the two legs on one side move first, and then the two on the other. Why is this important? Take a simple turn for example. If you ask your horse to turn left, and her left front foot is on the ground at the time you give seat, leg, and rein aids, it will be difficult for her to turn quickly or smoothly. If, however, you ask when her left front leg is off the ground and moving forward, she can easily pivot her forward movement to the left, and your turn will be smooth, tight, and balanced.

Watch your horse walk in the pasture. Pull up YouTube and watch many other horses walk. Then get on your horse and concentrate on the movement beneath you until you innately and instinctively know where the horse's legs are underneath you. You can thank me later for the improvement in your riding.

THE BACK IS ACTUALLY A REVERSE TROT.

I mentioned this a bit ago, but I still think it's cool that the horse's leg movement for both the trot and the back are in diagonal pairs: left front and right hind, and right front and left hind. Again, to fully understand how your horse's legs are moving, get down on all fours and do it yourself. Left arm and right leg, and right arm and left leg.

At the trot: left rear and right front together, and right rear and left front together in diagonal pairs.

Agnes just reminded me that some of you might find it difficult to get down onto the floor to try this, and might need something like a forklift to get back up (her words, not mine). If that's the case, you can do this same exercise from your chair, or from a standing position.

Once you have the movement down pat inside your head, you can concentrate on application. In addition to the turning aspect discussed at the walk, and still applicable at the trot, you have to know which diagonal pair of legs is off the ground to correctly do a posting, or rising, trot. For the uninitiated, this is when the rider moves up and down, in and out of the saddle, in rhythm to the horse's movement at the trot. Over distance, it is easier to post the trot than bounce along, which creates soreness in the horse's back, and in the rider's seat.

Here's how it works: Travelling in a circle clockwise, a rider should rise up out of the saddle when the left front/right rear diagonal pair is off the ground and moving forward. This helps balance the horse around turns—and helps balance the rider as well.

Building on the turning factor, when the rider only puts pressure on the rein to turn when the inside leg (the leg closest to the center of the circle) is off the ground, this puts the posting rider in a seated (and safer) position when asking the horse to turn. Admittedly, this takes some thought at first. To repeat, going clockwise, the rider would rise with the left front/right rear diagonal, and then sit and use the right rein and left leg aids when the right front/left rear diagonal pair of legs moves forward.

Reverse the aids when going the other direction, and remember to give yourself time to do the movements yourself and visualize it all in your head. If it's not clear now, it will be once you've practiced first on your own, and then with your horse.

When it comes to backing, especially when maneuvering out of a tight place on the trail, or between poles in an obstacle class, knowing which leg is moving when is vitally important. I once almost fell off a cliff when I asked my horse to back out of a trail that had dissipated into a mass of thorny brush. A steep hill was on my left, the path ahead had disintegrated to about three feet in width, and then the ground dropped off maybe ten feet to a stream below on my right. I was young, and didn't realize how critical it was to have control of my horse's right rear leg.

After backing no more than three steps, my horse almost backed into thin air. Fortunately, she stopped and refused to back any farther, and I was eventually smart enough to realize I needed to use a lot of right leg to move my horse's hind quarters back onto the hill side of the trail. If there had been room, I would have dismounted, but that was not possible here. Probably, you shouldn't ask how I got into that predicament in the first place.

THE LOPE/CANTER AND GALLOP REALLY ARE TWO DIFFERENT GAITS.
For a long time people questioned this. When a horse canters, or lopes, slowly, do his legs move in the same sequence as they do when he is running fast? I'd say yes . . . but then I'd be wrong.

Before you can understand the difference, you have to know a few things. First is terminology. Basically, the term canter is used when riding English. There are various styles of English riding, but think of the Olympic sports of Dressage and jumping, and you'll get the idea. The same gait is called a lope when riding western. Think cowboys and western movies. Okay, maybe the horse is moving a little less energetically at the lope than the canter, but the legs are moving in the same order.

The gallop is a faster, but similar gait, and we'll definitely get to it just as quick as green grass goes through a goose. (Best not to think too hard about that visual.)

Stride is something else we will discuss, and that is a full sequence of leg movements. Earlier we learned that when the horse walks, she moves her legs in this order: left rear, left front, right rear, right front. Each of these leg movements is a step, and together, all four leg movements at the walk are a stride.

Another important thing is the order in which the horse moves her legs at the canter (or lope), and that gets a little complicated, since it's different when the horse is moving to the left than to the right.

Both the canter/lope and the gallop, however, have a left lead and a right lead, meaning that one front leg moves farther forward than the other, and is thought of as a "leading" leg. Traveling clockwise, the legs at the canter move in the following order: left rear, then the right rear and left front move together as a diagonal pair, and then the right front. This constitutes a three-beat gait. Since two of the legs move together and a horse has four legs, there are three beats, or three steps, to the canter stride.

A left lead canter with the right rear, then the left rear and right front moving together as a diagonal pair, then the left front (the leading leg) moving forward.

You might want to stop and think about that for a bit. I remember learning all this when I was maybe fourteen and I can't tell you the number of hours I spent on my grandm<u>other's</u> front porch, chewing on a piece of grass, turning the movement of horse legs over and over in my mind. Maybe I'm slow, but it took me the better part of a summer to get it all down in my head, so don't feel badly if it takes you a while, too. I'm right there with you.

So again, clockwise: left rear, then the right rear and left front move together as a diagonal pair, and then the right front. Get that solidly in your mind, because now we're going to mix it up. Going the other way, counter-clockwise, we swap the left and right sides of the horse. Now the legs will move like this: right rear, left rear and right front as a diagonal pair, and left front. In addition to going through the motions yourself, it might help to watch a video, especially if you can look at a horse cantering in slow motion.

After watching some videos of horses loping along, try it yourself again, to see if it isn't easier. You will need a little more room than practicing at the walk and the trot. Your yard or driveway might suffice, or your riding arena, if you have one. First try a canter on the right lead by taking a step with your left leg. Then bring forward, together, your right leg and left arm (be sure they move together!), and then bring your right arm (your leading arm) forward. Best to start this slowly until you get the hang of it, and just disregard all the neighbors peeking out their curtains at you. Truly, you do not look silly. At all.

The reason for the difference in going to the left and to the right is that the horse needs the leading leg to be on the inside of whatever turn she is making to better balance herself—and you, if you are riding her.

Occasionally, a horse will cross-canter, and get the legs mixed up in some other order, usually something like left rear, right rear and right front, and then left front. Sit and think about that one for a while, too. Or get up, ignore the neighbors, and move through the sequence with your arms and legs. That's how all of this finally gelled for me.

The cross-canter can be quite uncomfortable to ride and, technically, it is not a lope or a canter since the definition of that gait requires there to be a diagonal pair of legs that move together. Lots of horses do this for a stride or two, whether being ridden or when out in the pasture playing with their friends, but then they get it together and get their legs straightened out and end up back in a true canter either on the left or right lead. A horse who cross-canters all the time might be arthritic, or have some other muscular-skeletal thing going on that could be cause for concern.

The gallop now, that's a bit of a different story. The gallop is a four-beat gait, with the front pair of legs hitting the ground separately, but in close sequence, and the rear pair of legs doing the same. The sequence of footfalls for a clockwise gallop would then be: left hind, right hind, left front, right front. The horse still starts with the hind leg that is to the outside of the circle and finishes the stride with the front leg that is closest to the inside of the circle.

Interestingly enough, the horse is not unique in her movement. Most four-legged mammals, including dogs, move in this manner. So go watch your dog walk and jog and lope. Technically, you could also watch your cat do the same, but they tend to be lazier and probably it will be a lot more effort on your part.

As Bubba says, "Why make a simple thing hard to do?"

I do not want to forget gaited horses here. These horses usually have an alternative gait to the trot, and sometimes to the walk as well. Just use the previous examples to process the movement of the gait: Understand which leg moves first and in what order the others follow. Practice it yourself. Solidify it in your mind, and then practice with your horse.

RIDING A HORSE MOVES A RIDER'S PELVIS IN A WAY THAT IS SIMILAR TO A HUMAN GAIT.
I confess. I don't exactly understand how it works, but riding does move your pelvis in a way that is similar to a human walking gait. Darcy might have more insight on this, since she is studying to become a therapeutic riding instructor. Or, do a Google search and read any of the many studies that have been done on this. All I know is that when a person rides, it helps them walk.

For example, Agnes is in her seventies and while I would never, ever say anything to her about it, I have noticed a teensy bit of a wobble in her gait. Not that everyone in their seventies and above wobbles when they walk, but some do, and Agnes is one of them. And I swear, if any of you say anything to her about it, well, we will have to have a different kind of conversation.

Anyway, if Agnes rode, which she won't, ever, because my goodness she is more scattered than confetti, I'd be afraid she'd confuse any horse she sat on, even kind, gentle Bob. But if she did ever ride, that wobble might disappear. Or at least improve some, or even stabilize and not deteriorate.

As best as I understand, the roll and pitch of the horse's pelvis causes our bodies to think we are walking, and we build muscle memory and muscle strength when we ride. So, anyone with cerebral palsy, a spinal cord injury, a traumatic brain injury, someone who has had a stroke—or any other condition that causes a person to walk poorly or unevenly—can have their walking improved by riding.

If you know someone like this (or maybe this is you), a therapeutic riding center is a good place to start. They have instructors who are extensively trained in horses, horsemanship, and a wide variety of disabilities, so they would know the best way to get started.

And seriously, forget all that I wrote about Agnes. Just forget it. She walks just fine. Really.

-THE END-

Acknowledgments

Cat Enright

Thank you to Jon, Darcy, and Bubba. No matter what happens, we will always be family. To Agnes, Carole, and Keith, you all are the best friends I could ever ask for. Dad and Marissa, you are always (okay, sometimes) in my thoughts. Petey, Bob, Gigi, and of course, Sally Blue, you all are my best horse friends and I can't express how much you mean to me. Hank, thank you for your howls that have protected me, and for lapping up crumbs off the kitchen floor after every meal. You are a good boy and I promise to let you (occasionally) bring your stick into the house. To Lisa, thank you for your friendship and for believing that my thoughts had enough value for a book. The writing process has been far more of a challenge than I ever expected, but I am really happy with the result. I hope you are, too. And finally, to Cool Titles, thank you for publishing this book, and for your support of the Cat Enright mystery series, and of me.

Lisa Wysocky

Cat Enright popped into my head in the middle of the night sometime around 1995. Since then, I have learned a lot about her and we have become good friends. I am not sure how that actually works, to be a friend with a fictional character, but there you go. Many thanks to Callie Rogers for help with the photos, and to Jenna Pratt, Ashley Hamblin, Kolby Noe Berry, Liz Mallard, Camden Branch, Kim Light, Jess Wilson, and Xander Altic for allowing Cat and me to use photos of them with the horses. Quincy, Tessie, Spike, and Lex: you are the best of the best. It is an absolute honor to get to work with you every day. Treats are coming, I promise. My sincere thanks go to Cat Enright for speaking so clearly inside my head for so many years, to Neville and Cindy Johnson at Cool Titles (the very best book publisher I could ever imagine for the Cat Enright cozy equestrian mystery series), and to you, the reader. So many readers have become (almost) as enamored of Cat and her world as I am, and have learned about horses along the way. You are the wind beneath our wings and I cannot thank you enough.

Author Bios

Cat Enright

Cat Enright was born in Chicago, but before she turned ten, she moved to rural Bucksnort, Tennessee to live with her maternal grandmother. This was after her mother died and her father found solace in the bottle. She says the horses at a riding stable down the road saved her, and she ended up earning a B.S. in equine management from Middle Tennessee State University. Shortly after graduation her grandmother passed, and Cat used the $55,000 in cash that she found stuffed under her grandmother's mattress for a down payment on twenty acres in Ashland City, Tennessee, near Nashville. She put stalls in the old tobacco barn on the property and moved into the old farmhouse, and hung out her shingle. Ten years later, Cat has amassed several dozen national and world champion Appaloosa wins, and trained many national champion riders. She likes horses better than people, only cooks cold cereal and hot chocolate, and has a habit of stumbling over dead bodies. Learn more at Facebook.com/CatEnrightMysteryHorsewoman

Lisa Wysocky

Lisa Wysocky is an award-winning author, editor, podcaster, equine clinician, and motivational speaker who trains horses for and consults with therapeutic riding programs. She has also been chosen as one of the country's Top 50 riding instructors by ARIA (American Riding Instructor's Association). Among many other books, Lisa is the author of the award-winning Cat Enright equestrian mystery series, and as a speaker and horse expo clinician teaches ground driving, form to function, balanced riding, resistance-free leading, and life skills learned from the horse herd. She is the host of seasons two and three of *The Horse Nutrition Podcast, Presented by Purina*, and the *Celebs with Horses* podcast. She also is a regular substitute co-host of the *Horses in the Morning* podcast. All air on the Horse Radio Network (now part of the Equine Network family) and on podcast players everywhere. Lisa also serves as executive director of the nonprofit organization Colby's Army, and in her fifteen minutes of spare time each year enjoys hiking, gardening, water sports, playing Scrabble, Minnesota Twins baseball . . . and reading. She splits her time between Tennessee and Minnesota. Find her online at LisaWysocky.com

**Learn more about the Cat Enright mysteries
with these first five books in the series.**

The Opium Equation

When retired movie star Glenda Dupree was murdered at her antebellum mansion near Nashville, Tennessee, there was much speculation, but no one missed her much. Prior to leaving life on earth, Glenda had managed to offend everyone in sight, including her neighbor, a (mostly) law-abiding horse trainer named Cat Enright. Cat is implicated in the murder, and also in the disappearance of a ten-year-old neighbor, Bubba Henley. Cat thinks Bubba's disappearance ties into the murder and realizes her name will not be cleared until he is found. With the help of her riding students, a (possibly) psychic horse, a local cop, a kid named Frog, and an eccentric client of a certain age with electric blue hair, Cat takes time from her horse training business to try to solve the case and keep herself out of prison.

The Magnum Equation

A horse trainer, juvenile delinquent, eccentric client of a certain age with electric blue hair, and a (possibly) psychic horse lead this Southern equestrian mystery into a fast paced, lightly comic read. Join Cat Enright and her crew as she tries to solve murder and mayhem at a prestigious all-breed horse show. When horses become ill and a show-goer's last hurrah is in the port-a-potty, Cat decides to find the cause of the trouble.

The Fame Equation

Tennessee horse trainer Cat Enright pushes the boundaries of lost friendships as she tries to solve the murder of a country music star. When the body is found floating down the river from a nearby therapeutic riding center, Cat dives into the investigation. Between mourning a friend, chasing down murderers, an absent boyfriend, a new horse, an extra child, learning the ways of the music industry, and the weird behavior of the (possibly) psychic mare Sally Blue, Cat has her hands full.

The Mane Equation

Cat Enright finds herself at Canterbury Park in Minnesota after her estranged father, a groom at the track, insists someone is trying to kill him. Cat is happy to temporarily leave her newly-complicated life to see what is going on. After one jockey goes missing and another is murdered, Cat finds herself calling on friends in Tennessee to keep her dad and herself safe. One by one, Jon, Darcy, Bubba, Agnes, and even the possibly psychic horse Sally Blue, help Cat discover the truth.

The Rein Equation

At a competitive trail competition Cat Enright finds the body of one of the riders, which ultimately causes Cat to doubt her closest friends and neighbors. When hunky country music star Keith Carson saves Cat's life, she struggles to remember details that can point her toward the killer—before the killer comes for her. Aided by her usual eclectic cast, including the (possibly) psychic mare, Sally Blue, if Cat wins in the end, she may lose what she loves the most.

All photos courtesy of Lisa Wysocky with the exception of the photo of Lex and the feed tub, and of Spike pinning his ears. Those credits go to Callie Rogers.

The photo on the opposite page? We're not sure where that came from or how it got into this book, but we have a sneaking suspicion it is a photo of a certain (possibly) psychic mare.

www.ingramcontent.com/pod-product-compliance
Lightning Source LLC
LaVergne TN
LVHW020933090426
835512LV00020B/3338